RENEWALS 458-4574

DATE DUE

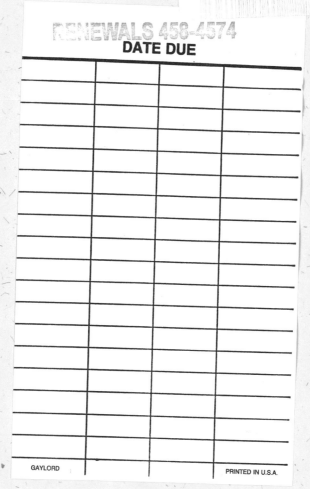

GAYLORD   PRINTED IN U.S.A.

Reviewer Quotes for
The Solution-Centric Organization

"This book is a must-read for managers or executives that are looking for a fresh approach to old sales and marketing issues. The issues and challenges discussed in *The Solution-Centric Organization* are right on track with the rapidly evolving market environment of today. If companies are going to add value through differentiation, they must find a way to systemically build an enterprise that can integrate sales and marketing with the new solution-centric discipline that the authors outline step by step."

PAUL R. BLOCK
CHAIRMAN AND CEO, MERISANT WORLDWIDE, INC.

"Until now, integrating solution-centric thinking throughout the organization (to support the solution focus) has been left to individual sales professionals and their managers. *The Solution-Centric Organization* provides a jumpstart for building a significant sustainable, solution-centric advantage."

JOHN A. WEBER
PROFESSOR OF MARKETING
UNIVERSITY OF NOTRE DAME

"The fact that sales organizations must transition from being product-centric to solution-centric is clear to virtually all CSOs; how to do it is not! What we need today is for someone to cut through all the hype about getting closer to our customers, and show us how to do it. Eades and Kear are those visionaries, and *The Solution-Centric Organization* is that roadmap to change. They provide a step-by-step map for how to navigate this paradigm shift in order to turn 'how you sell' into a sustainable competitive advantage."

JIM DICKIE
FOUNDER, CSO INSIGHTS

"In this day and age—with global competitors coming frequently and from all directions—this book is a must-read for anyone in the company executive suite. Often executives like ideas and concepts but have little or no idea on how to start moving forward. This book gives executives both the ideas as to how to proceed—and the practical steps for getting the transformation process underway."

RICK RAMSDEN
FORMER MANAGING PARTNER,
PRICEWATERHOUSECOOPERS CONSULTING

"Post-2000 buying patterns have changed the ground rules to compete and win and thus the term 'solution-centric' has a very different meaning in today's marketplace. Competitive differentiation today from a 'product' perspective is short lived—true long-term 'customer value' must be delivered with intellectual capital and become the 'DNA' of the company. This book gets the message across in an enlightened way for the reader."

J.G. LICATA, JR.
PRESIDENT, SIEMENS ENTERPRISE NETWORKS

"*The Solution-Centric Organization* offers a strategy that every organization can apply to escape the commodity trap. Instead of focusing on products, their features, and how great they may be, the successful seller must focus on customers, their needs, and how products can be linked to provide value-enhancing solutions for customers. Doing this successfully requires a fundamental corporate reorientation, and Eades and Kear offer practical methods and techniques to make this transformation."

BRUCE YANDLE
DEAN AND PROFESSOR OF ECONOMICS EMERITUS
COLLEGE OF BUSINESS & BEHAVIORAL SCIENCE
CLEMSON UNIVERSITY

"The book defines a new global environment where continuation of existing B2B business models around marketing and sales are becoming ineffective.... The message of this book is much more strategic than tactical, with huge implications that will impact the success of business in the future. The authors are probably onto one of the primary causes of flat growth and earnings projections for many companies."

RON COX
FORMER CEO, ACHIEVEGLOBAL

THE SOLUTION-CENTRIC ORGANIZATION

KEITH M. EADES
ROBERT E. KEAR

McGraw-Hill

New York   Chicago   San Francisco
Lisbon   London   Madrid   Mexico City
Milan   New Delhi   San Juan   Seoul
Singapore   Sydney   Toronto

The **McGraw·Hill** Companies

1 2 3 4 5 6 7 8 9 10   DOC/DOC   0 9 8 7 6

ISBN 0-07-226264-8

This publication is designed to provide accurate and authoritative information in regard to the subject matter covered. It is sold with the understanding that neither the author nor the publisher is engaged in rendering legal, accounting, futures/securities trading, or other professional service. If legal advice or other expert assistance is required, the services of a competent professional person should be sought.

> —*From a Declaration of Principles jointly adopted*
> *by a Committee of the American Bar Association*
> *and a Committee of Publishers*

McGraw-Hill books are available at special quantity discounts to use as premiums and sales promotions, or for use in corporate training programs. For more information, please write to the Director of Special Sales, Professional Publishing, McGraw-Hill, Two Penn Plaza, New York, NY 10121-2298. Or contact your local bookstore.

 This book is printed on recycled, acid-free paper containing a minimum of 50% recycled, de-inked fiber.

Contents

Foreword

THANKS TO AN EVER-GROWING INFRASTRUCTURE to support the worldwide instantaneous availability of information, the globalization of markets is accelerating. And yet, too many businesses fail to recognize the incredible opportunities and potential threats posed by this unstoppable trend. Globalization creates worldwide markets eager to acquire new goods and services heretofore unavailable or very limited to them, but it also increases the pressure of competition by many orders of magnitude. No longer can businesspeople hide comfortably in their isolated local markets—the world's market is now inescapably a global one.

As a result, the pressure to differentiate oneself from a growing number of worldwide alternatives is also increasing. Many businesses are trying to do this by bundling "a little of this with a little of that," so to speak, and by proclaiming that these assemblies of features or services are "solutions," as if this word were some kind of magical tonic for warding off the looming menace of commoditization. As Keith Eades and Robert Kear point out in this book, this "pseudo-solution" approach doesn't work very well, if at all. Instead, they have recognized that to compete effectively in today's global market, organizations need to first change something much more fundamental: the way that they perceive themselves and their customers.

As a global company, we at Hitachi Data Systems recognized the dual-edged sword of globalization quickly. For many years, we have enjoyed our well-earned reputation for providing state-of-the-art technology products to our customers, and we support this with world-class service. We realized, however, that we could maintain our leadership position only by overcoming the ever-increasing pressures of commoditization and global competition. We have succeeded by shifting our focus from being product-centric to solution-centric. Today, we define ourselves not just by the products or services that we offer, but by how we can solve our customers' problems—and this is beginning to have an impact on everything we undertake as a business.

This book is all about how to succeed in today's tough marketplace by transitioning your organization to solution-centricity, just as we have. Eades and Kear provide insightful ideas about how organizations can adjust their thinking in order to better solve the problems of customers and thereby differentiate themselves from commoditized offerings. Further, the authors provide practical tools and methods for analyzing your own organization's barriers to solution-centric transformation and helpful advice about how to overcome these barriers.

As Hitachi Data Systems succeeds in establishing itself as a world-leading solution-centric company, these concepts play an important role in our transformation. As you read *The Solution-Centric Organization*, I encourage you to apply these ideas for improving your own organization's competitiveness and ability to provide value to customers.

—Dave Roberson
President and CEO, Hitachi Data Systems

Introduction

IN 1988, ONE OF US, KEITH EADES, founded Sales Performance International (SPI), a sales consulting and training firm dedicated to improving clients' ability to sell and generate revenue. After nearly two decades, SPI's consultants have worked with hundreds of organizations and trained over 600,000 salespeople, managers, and executives in a sales methodology called Solution Selling®, which enabled sales teams to differentiate themselves not only by *what* they sold but, more importantly, by *how* they sold to customers. (For more about Solution Selling principles, pick up a copy of *The New Solution Selling: The Revolutionary Sales Process That Is Changing the Way People Sell*, published by McGraw-Hill, 2004.)

During the same time period, the other one of us, Robert Kear, managed marketing teams in several rapidly growing, high-technology companies. He observed that when salespeople engaged with customers, they often focused extensively on features and functions of products rather than on how those capabilities solved customers' problems. In the high-demand economic period prior to 2000, the ability to present product and service capabilities was usually sufficient for salespeople to be successful. However, the post-2000 economic climate has created a more discerning customer. In this relatively lower-demand environment, it has become far more critical for salespeople to position and defend the value and differentiation of their offerings. In addition, just to *earn* the right to engage in selling activities often requires a compelling, relevant message to cut through the white noise of the marketplace because of the information avalanche that customers are increasingly experiencing.

What Robert began to observe in this environment was the extent to which marketing organizations had become acclimated to the demand-rich, product-centric era prior to 2000. A concurrent observation was the degree to which this product-centric mindset was misaligned with sales improvement initiatives that focused exclusively on retooling the sales force to sell "value" or solutions, versus products and services. Robert began to think extensively about how *marketing* could better align its thinking and methods to provide the sales force with messages, "air cover," and tools that concentrated on positioning value effectively, versus product superiority and features.

Independently, we each discovered that both marketing and sales methods can play a material role in what takes place at the point-of-sales interaction. However, we also discovered that organizational resistance and corporate "silos" often constrained the degree of *sustainable* performance improvement. In plain language, both training salespeople and developing solution messaging helped performance, but the amount of improvement was limited if sales was not *formally* aligned with marketing, or vice versa, or if the organization's executive team didn't manage and support these projects and make them an ongoing way of conducting business.

When we met in 2004, we discovered that we were looking at the same problem from different viewpoints—sales and marketing organizations both have an integral role to play in the transition to becoming providers of real solutions to customers' business problems, not just vendors of products. We both realized that each of us was trying to address the issue from a "localized" viewpoint—one focused on sales, the other on marketing. If we could combine these approaches into a comprehensive, systemic marketing and sales framework, then companies could significantly improve the probabilities of winning profitable business on a more consistent basis. This book is the result of that research and collaboration effort. In these pages, you'll find a systemic approach to helping companies evolve their "revenue engine" from being product-centric to solution-centric and therefore become better equipped to compete successfully in today's global marketplace.

But we all know that it's not enough just to be better equipped, or even to better integrate sales and marketing. The key question that still remains is, "How do we drive these solution-centric concepts into the culture of our organization—how do we make it a way of life?" In the course of developing the material for this book, we have discovered that the path to solution-centricity requires an evolutionary—if not revolutionary—way of new thinking across the entire organization. Just as Six Sigma, total quality management (TQM), business reengineering, just-in-time manufacturing, and other business transformation ideas require fundamental changes in both organizational mindset and action in order to reap their promised rewards, so does the transformation from being product-centric to solution-centric.

WHO NEEDS TO READ THIS BOOK?

Anyone who is interested in driving sales performance improvement—and making the customer the center of everything his or her organization does—will find value in this book. Becoming solution-centric is an organizational transformation, requiring teamwork and alignment in every part of the company. As a result, not only will executives find the contents of this book of interest, many other departmental managers will also find it useful, including:

- *Marketing professionals.* Embracing solution-centricity has significant implications for how marketing specialists think and act. The kinds of messages that they produce—and how they use those messages to communicate internally and to customers—change dramatically when an organization becomes solution-centric.

- *Sales professionals.* The words that come out of the sales channel's mouth and into your customer's ears at the point of purchase are some of the most important if the organization is to be perceived as solution-centric. The actions of a successful solution-centric sales organization are also radically different than of those that are product-centric.

- *Customer service and support.* All the positioning and posturing in the world won't mean a thing if the solution-centric view stops in the customer service department. Organizations that want customers' long-term business must also align the way their service and support teams interact with customers if they want to reap the full benefits of solution-centricity. While this book does not directly address the customer service function, it should be possible for readers to extrapolate appropriate practices for service functions from many of the concepts presented herein.
- *Operational managers and executives.* If you are a manager or executive in your organization, you can benefit from knowing how to support your organization's efforts to become solution-centric. If you are in finance or administration, for example, knowing how your department's policies align with a solution-centric orientation can make a material difference in your company's success.
- *Partners and alliances.* Many companies form partnerships or alliances with third-party organizations so that they can provide better solutions to joint customers. If your partner or ally is a solution-centric organization, then you need to understand the values your partner is using to make decisions so that you can maximize the value you gain from the relationship.

If your success is dependent upon either your ability or your organization's ability to market, sell, and deliver high-value solutions, then this book is for you.

NAVIGATING THIS BOOK

This book is organized into four parts, and each part is divided into several chapters. We recommend that you read the book sequentially, as each part builds upon ideas expressed previously.

It is important to understand one other aspect of how this book was developed. Often books of this type provide useful ideas and concepts but leave the readers to their own devices in terms of taking meaningful action. The intent of this book is to both provide a context of key concepts and principles for solution-centricity, as well as provide a practical framework for taking action within your organization.

To that end, the first three parts of the book provide a traditional reading experience, where concepts and ideas related to solution-centric transformation are presented. However, Part Four is somewhat different; here we provide a comprehensive set of assessment criteria that can actually be used by your organization to evaluate where potential sales performance gaps exist. In addition, this section of the book also provides numerous templates and tools that can be applied to adopt a more solution-centric approach. In other words, in Part Four of the book, we delve deeply into the practical details of *how* to make the transition to being solution-centric.

The four parts of the book are organized as follows:

- *Part One: A New Sales Environment.* This section makes the case for transforming into a solution-centric organization. It describes the emerging focus on solution-centricity, the growing trend on solutions focus, and common reactions to sales performance problems in business today.

- *Part Two: Solution-Centric Concepts and Principles.* This part describes the essential principles of solution-centricity and how to embrace them. It explores the dangers of pseudo-solutions, describes the implications for sales, and explains the kinds of organizational transformations needed to become solution-centric.

- *Part Three: A Practical Framework to Drive Performance Improvement.* This section describes a systemic approach for aligning marketing and sales functions to support solution-centric behavior, and how to integrate those activities to improve revenue generation.

- *Part Four: Sales Performance Health Check.* This section provides a practical assessment methodology for objectively determining where systemic factors are most likely having a negative impact on overall sales performance. In addition to presenting fundamental assessment criteria for each of 24 performance areas, Part Four also includes numerous templates and tools that can help to establish improved rigor in the understanding of customer problems and needs. In addition, many of these templates and tools help to create a common, solution-centric frame of reference and language between marketing and sales that can help to align and drive the corporate revenue engine.

Before we proceed any further, please note this is not primarily a research book about becoming and being solution-centric. We don't extensively compare and contrast groups of companies and then isolate a set of behaviors or principles that separate the "good" companies from the "bad" companies. It's not that these types of books aren't valuable or informative. There are literally dozens of well-written and well-researched business books that examine successful and less successful companies and then correlate success criteria with certain practices and principles. While we utilize some research to illustrate key points or to support concepts about solution-centricity, this book is oriented more to the future—to a future state you desire for your organization and, more importantly, to a practical approach for how to get there.

In our experience working with hundreds of corporations for almost two decades, companies need more than collections of ideas and principles from "successful" peers, because many transformational concepts can be so all-encompassing that companies don't know how to take meaningful, prioritized action.

Our goal here is to be more practical and definitive—to rescue the term *solution-centric* from the fate of *customer-centric*.

Think for a moment about the customer-centric movement. There have been so many articles, books, white papers, discussion threads, blogs, and seminars about customer-centricity that the term has been rendered almost meaningless. It's not that there aren't good ideas to be found in this content—it's that there are so many perspectives and nuances of what it means to be customer-centric that companies are left to fashion their own interpretations and courses of action. So what usually happens in this situation? We've all been there. Typically there is some executive declaration about the bold new company philosophy, posters appear in every hallway, and the organization embarks on a variety of projects and initiatives that are going to "transform the company." But a year or two later, little has actually *systemically* changed the "DNA" of the company. That's unfortunate because some of the core ideas about customer-centricity are very valuable.

Our goal here is to be more practical and definitive—to rescue the term *solution-centric* from the fate of *customer-centric*. In this case, less is more. What companies don't need is a thousand ideas, opinions, and perspectives about how to become more solution-focused. Instead, companies that are legitimately striving to become solution-centric need practical "recipes" and specific methods to realign their businesses. That is, they need a *finite* number of alignment concepts and principles and a corresponding set of actual steps they can take to transform key aspects of their revenue engine.

This is where the term *solution-centric* has an advantage over the term *customer-centric*, because we can define the former more narrowly—which we will do later in this book. This definition allows us to create a *manageable* set of alignment principles, primarily in sales and marketing, that lead to an actual methodology for systemic transformation.

So we're not attempting to identify *every* facet of what it means to be solution-centric here. Such an initiative would likely require multiple volumes and years. For almost 20 years, we have been helping major corporations make a fundamental transformation—from selling products to selling solutions. In this book, we attempt to focus on a manageable starting point that entails key aspects of corporate transformation that directly impact the *revenue engine*—the ability to consistently market and sell high-value offerings that address real customer problems and needs. But here's the irony—after years of training thousands of salespeople in hundreds of companies to *sell* solutions, we've discovered there is much more to effectively selling real solutions than simply educating the sales force.

While investments in sales training and process integration pay significant dividends, many companies are interested in getting to an even higher level. They ask, "How can we integrate and extend the principles of Solution Selling more broadly into our overall business model to increase the probabilities of sustained sales growth?"—in essence, "What is the *corporate methodology* for selling solutions?" We address that question in this book.

In our years of experience across multiple organizations, we have discovered numerous holistic factors that can contribute significantly to effective Solution Selling. In two previous books, one of our authors, Keith, focused on process and behavior changes solely within the sales organization (*The New Solution Selling*, McGraw-Hill, 2004) and on practical tools, application exercises, templates, and scripts (*The Solution Selling Fieldbook*,

McGraw-Hill, 2005) to help salespeople and companies apply the Solution Selling approach to be more effective at sales execution. In this book, we delve more deeply into the systemic, cross-functional factors that enable Solution Selling excellence across the organization—the consistent ability to make the best possible connections with the most appropriate buyers during sales interactions.

The earlier books explained how to sell solutions through a consultative selling approach that diagnosed a customer's problems and framed the answer to those problems as an integrated solution. When we ask the sales force to become more consultative, however, we must also pose the questions: "How can we become a better problem-solving organization?" and "How do we provide direction and support to salespeople continuously and synergistically across the organization so the impact of the interaction with buyers is the best it can be?" The challenge in accomplishing this is in framing a realistic set of principles for making the transformation to solution-centric behavior and in defining an approach to change that is at the same time systemic but also practical and achievable.

BEGINNING YOUR JOURNEY

You are about to be challenged. While the potential rewards for becoming solution-centric—significant competitive advantage, larger sales volumes, increased revenue and profits, higher employee morale, and increased customer loyalty—are highly attractive, the potential obstacles can be daunting. Solution-centricity is a significant organizational transformation, and realistically, most established companies have decades of product-centric DNA to overcome. We are immersed in a world of product-centric dinosaurs, many of whom are in denial about the impending "commodity wars" of the global economy. The question to answer for your organization is, "Are you one of them?"

This book provides a practical means for understanding what it takes to begin the transition to solution-centricity. It also provides a foundation that your organization can successfully build upon and evolve to better exploit the unique opportunities in your markets. The demand-rich era has past—the time to begin this transformation is now.

Acknowledgments

While we are the named authors of this book, in reality the book is the result of the collaborative work and research of many talented and knowledgeable individuals. Of particular note is Tim Sullivan—not only is Tim a published author in his own right, he is one of the world's foremost authorities in sales disciplines and methodologies. In addition, Dave Davies provided significant input in methodology-related areas. We would also like to extend a special thanks to Bob Sanchez, CEO of Sales Performance International, for underwriting the human and intellectual capital and many other resources required for developing this book.

We also owe special thanks to Jimmy Touchstone, Michael Bier, and Andrew Plunkett for their contributions to the book manuscript and their methodology expertise. Special gratitude also goes to Jeffrey Krames and Roger Stewart at McGraw-Hill. They both shared our vision for the book and helped bring it to market.

Last but not least, we want to thank our families and the staff at Sales Performance International for their tireless help and support throughout the writing of this book.

Thank you all.

Keith Eades
Robert Kear

P A R T
O N E

A NEW SALES ENVIRONMENT

A FOCUS ON SOLUTION-CENTRICITY

*There is much more to effectively selling
real solutions than simply educating
the sales force.*

When the CEO *has an earnings call every 90 days, and the average tenure for a chief sales officer is 22 months,* systemic *is a frightening word.*

WHAT IS SOLUTION-CENTRIC?

In short, being solution-centric means that your organization defines itself by the problems you solve for customers, versus by the products or services *you* make, sell, or deliver. In a solution-centric organization, every aspect of the company—from marketing to research and development to manufacturing to sales to customer service—operates in harmony with how customers need to solve their real problems. Solution-centric organizations gauge their value not just by the amount of revenue or earnings they attain, but also by the results and positive outcomes that their customers achieve through using their goods and services.

Solution-centric organizations still have to sell products and services—and product features or service capabilities are still important. But features and capabilities are only relevant to the extent that they *directly* contribute to positive outcomes for customers. Solution-centric organizations recognize that they cannot rely solely on their products to sustain growth and profitability. They must also stand apart from competitive alternatives by the *integrated* way that they market, sell, deliver, and provide service for offerings that address the critical problems and needs of customers.

WHY IS BEING SOLUTION-CENTRIC IMPORTANT?

In the robust economic period during the two decades prior to 2000, most organizations could do quite well leading with their products or services. Budgets were flush, and corporations were *investment* oriented. For example, in business-to-business transactions, most organizations could achieve their revenue goals by selling to middle managers and focusing on product features and functions. As long as they could demonstrate how their wares performed, and supply the needed goods at the right time and the right price, salespeople could close enough business with midlevel buyers to meet corporate goals and maintain individual quota levels.

Post-2000, and especially post-9/11, everything is different. We now live in a world of heightened uncertainty. It is far more difficult to confidently predict future events and economic trends. Long-term confidence has been replaced with short-term concerns about risk and consequences for making the wrong decision. Today, buyers are more cautious, and buying committee size has increased significantly in the past five years. Budgets are leaner, and decisions about capital expenditures are made at higher levels—in the executive suite in many cases. Not surprisingly, overall sales quota attainment has slipped significantly in the post-2000 economic environment.

As a result, organizations can no longer rely on product features or service capabilities alone to sell their offerings. They must be capable of effectively marketing and selling value—the ability to address customers' most pressing business problems. In addition, they must be increasingly capable of connecting effectively with top-of-mind issues and challenges of key executives. To succeed in today's uncertain environment, organizations must become solution-centric.

INDIVIDUAL COMBATANTS DON'T WIN WARS; ARMIES DO.

WE CAN'T HANDLE THE TRUTH

Sales effectiveness is rarely a *localized* problem, and most seasoned executives grasp this reality. But organizational behavior often parallels human behavior. We call this the *crash diet syndrome.* We all know there is overwhelming statistical evidence that crash diets fail to deliver sustainable weight loss. But remarkably, a multibillion dollar industry continues to thrive on a simple hope: "If I can just lose that first 10 pounds fast, then I'll be on my way." All this occurs when we know full well that sustainable weight loss requires a much more fundamental transformation—a systemic change in multiple aspects of lifestyle.

As in the case of the promises of miracle diets, we continue to be amazed at the wishful thinking of many companies experiencing growth or sales performance problems. Executives at these companies seem to *hope* their growth problems are localized or are isolated to a few simple "levers," primarily in the sales organization.

Of course, in many cases the sales organization's issues and problems *are* contributing to the shortfall. It's not that improvement initiatives like sales training don't help—sales training to a business is as essential as boot camp is to the foot soldier. But, sales training cannot single-handedly carry the initiative. Individual combatants don't win wars; armies do. Behind every modern-day soldier lays a vast systemic support system that provides initial training, continued learning and reinforcement, standardized methods and practices, up-to-date critical information and direction, continuous logistical support, and technology assistance—all *aligned* around the goal of optimizing the effectiveness of each combatant and optimizing the effectiveness of the whole army. Battles are typically won or lost due to a combination of multiple factors.

Similarly, in selling, the difference between winning and losing is rarely the result of a single factor. The research firm Primary Intelligence (www.primary-intel.com) has performed thousands of win-loss analyses, and its studies vividly illustrate this point. The sales performance trap lies in confusing *symptoms* with the actual *causes* for performance breakdowns. Most companies invest in improvement, but as Rob Jeppsen, chief strategy officer of Primary Intelligence, notes, "Our research indicates that most of the time, companies guess wrong about why they aren't winning more often."

In many cases, the causal factors are highly systemic, and sustainable change on the front lines, at the point of buyer interaction, requires a real understanding of key alignment requirements—ranging from the initial value proposition itself all the way through to the precise circumstances at the point of sale. As the research firm IDC so aptly noted recently, "The days of the lone-wolf sales star are over." In other words, these days optimizing your organization's ability to sell solutions is about alignment—it's about *configuring and calibrating* key aspects of marketing and sales execution to optimize effectiveness. In our world, that means configuring the process from end to end and calibrating or tuning specific aspects of marketing and sales execution around an actual solution-centric *methodology* or a framework for sales performance improvement.

> In most cases, companies simply don't know why they aren't winning more often.

While this book does not delve deeply into engineering or manufacturing, we do briefly discuss the role that methodology can play to drive appropriate priorities and solution "definitions" for those areas as well. Taking a systemic view doesn't mean you have to boil the ocean or make enormous capital investments. *But if you want to be exceptional at selling high-value solutions, you have to genuinely understand where the primary levers for transformation reside in your organization and commit to aligning them.*

So why is the quick fix so appealing? Why do people and companies avoid confronting what they know is rational and true? Most of us don't really believe diet pills are going to work. Similarly, most senior executives recognize sales revenues probably aren't going to improve significantly by simply providing a single refresher event or even a one-time "boot camp" for the sales force. So why is that approach such a common phenomenon in business?

In part, we don't confront what we know to be true because getting to the truth is often painful—avoidance is more comfortable. Unless the pain is severe, the status quo or path of least resistance is often the course of action. But perhaps more importantly, the attractiveness of the diet pill or the training event lies in their conceptual simplicity and speed. They provide a *simple and quick* way to take some form of action in a world where complexity and patience are the enemies of action. When we realize a legitimate lifestyle change might take several years, the diet pill is enormously seductive. When we realize a problem is systemic by nature and that a solution has many interdependencies, it can be intimidating at both a personal and organizational level. When the CEO has an earnings call every 90 days, and the average tenure for a chief sales officer is 22 months, *systemic* is a frightening word.

Without legitimate frameworks to reduce the complexity of systemic transformation, many companies continue to take simple forms of isolated and quick action. Or they resort to cross-silo finger pointing when things aren't going well. It isn't that systemic dependencies aren't recognized; it's that no structured, formal framework for addressing critical cross-functional issues is in place. Without such a framework, there is no way of aligning activities, and organizational boundaries and politics take over. New "sand castles" are often created by isolated projects or visionaries, but the pace of business washes them away in short order. Then it's back to business as usual—just like the yo-yo crash diet syndrome.

What people and companies need are practical frameworks and methodologies that help reduce the complexity of systemic change. They need methods and tools that help them to quit guessing wrong about what is broken and what needs to change. In addition, they need to know more than what has to be accomplished; they need practical guidelines on how to actually make the necessary changes.

In this book, we'll show you just such a structured, formal framework for addressing the critical cross-functional issues that shape your organization's sales performance.

SO WHO IS SOLUTION-CENTRIC?

When we were first approached to write this book, we were asked, "Who are some of the companies today that best exemplify a 'solution-centric' organization?" On the surface this question sounds like an easy one to answer— after all, there is clearly no shortage of companies *claiming* to provide solutions in today's marketplace.

For example, recently several management consulting firms identified companies who have, from the perspective of the management consulting firms, been able to execute a solutions strategy with some degree of effectiveness (we will briefly touch on some of this research later). However, while varying levels of solution-oriented practices exist, we haven't been able to locate a "poster child" company to *thoroughly* illustrate the overall criteria for solution-centricity presented in this book. With so many companies claiming to provide solutions, why is this?

Primarily, it's because the definition of what it means to provide a solution is so rampantly abused or widely interpreted. After 15 years of working with companies attempting to move from selling products to selling solutions, we've reached the conclusion that the basic concepts of what it means to be solution-focused or to be a solution-centric organization are almost universally misunderstood, and in a big way. In large part, product-centricity is so engrained in the DNA of most companies that to escape it successfully requires a fundamental rethinking of the corporation. In essence, old habits and ways of thinking die very hard—especially when a company has been relatively successful in the past.

In their book, *Markets of One*, Joe Pine and David Gilmore noted the following about the promise of mass customization:

> Customers have grown so accustomed to established industry practices that they no longer expect any alternative—let alone one that's exactly what they want.

It is precisely this preconditioned mindset that the authors see as a "great impediment" to innovation. While the context of their book is about mass customization, the point is well taken—in many cases companies and their customers (and markets) need to be "jolted" by a truly new approach to solving problems or they will continue to follow traditional patterns of behavior. A recent discussion with an executive illustrated this point vividly. The following paragraph paraphrases the key points of the conversation.

> Our customers and prospects are sophisticated and already understand the problems we are solving for them. We typically respond to RFPs that have been prepared by industry experts. Industry analysts essentially control the buying criteria, and we are compelled to deliver the features that analysts indicate are essential. There's a fairly large addressable market, and as long as we get our fair share, we'll do reasonably well.

In other words, the mold for the industry and offering has been set; the rules have been defined; and we are compelled to play by the rules. At face value, this may seem like an incredibly fatalistic viewpoint. But how common is this general point of view? In our observations across hundreds of companies in the past decade, this mindset is fairly typical. The perspective can be summarized as follows:

1. We provide products or services to buyers that already understand the need and value of our offerings.
2. Customers know we are a provider of these types of products, and the perceived superiority of our offering

is what typically provides the winning edge. That is, if we can successfully address more of the requirements of the customer, we have a good chance of winning.

3. In some cases, a relationship can offset the shortcomings of our products or open a door; however, with greater budgetary scrutiny and larger buying committees the relationship sell has become less of a factor.

In other words, as soon as markets become fairly well defined, an assumptive mentality begins to set in—of course customers know *why* they need our product, don't they?

But what happens when companies stop doing reasonably well? What happens when the traditional way of competing for business begins to be less effective? What typically occurs when win rates start to decline, sales cycles elongate, and quota attainment drops? In many cases what often sets in is what we call the "riptide" effect—companies basically try to *swim harder* in the same direction. The key to surviving a riptide is counterintuitive—if you swim directly toward shore, you will actually lose ground and eventually drown, regardless of how hard or long you swim. You have to understand that you are in a *fundamentally* different situation than you have been in the past, and swimming parallel to shore before swimming in is the only route to safety.

The "riptide" effect—swimming harder in the same direction—is increasingly becoming a prescription for failure.

And so companies that have competed successfully for 20 or more years often resolve to "execute" their way out of a sales decline. Like a riptide victim, they try to swim harder in the same direction. Studies conducted across several hundred major corporations by CSO Insights (www.csoinsights.com) indicated that in 1999, quota attainment levels in several vertical industry segments were at nearly 70 percent. However, post-2002, quota attainment has struggled to move out of the 50 to 60 percent range and reached a low of 49 percent in 2004. Jim Dickie, founder of CSO Insights, commented on the slight improvement in quota attainment that his company observed in its 2005 report on sales effectiveness (see Figure 1.1).

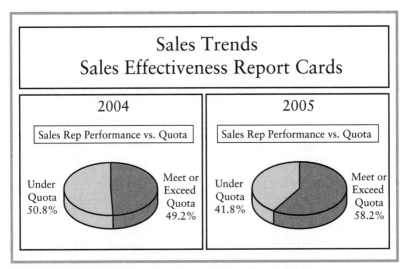

Figure 1.1 CSO Insights' Report on Sales Effectiveness
Source: CSO Insights, "State of the Marketplace Review," 2004–2005.

While there was an improvement from 2004 to 2005 in quota attainment—there was not a corresponding improvement in overall effectiveness metrics—it appears to primarily be a result of sales forces simply working harder, and this type of improvement is not sustainable.

In addition, data from the fourth quarter is pointing to marginal, if any, improvement in quota attainment for the current year. In other words, companies seem to be stuck on a treadmill of sorts when it comes to sustainable progress in sales performance improvement.

But wait—aren't many companies taking a fundamentally different approach by becoming more solutions-focused? You be the judge. If you don't think the product-centric "feature/function" mindset is alive and well, just visit a few thousand Web sites. Later in the book, we will present a high-level analysis of several hundred corporate Web sites. Whether business-to-business (B2B) or business-to-consumer (B2C) related, how many of them actually delve into specifics about customer problems, challenges, and needs? We don't mean a list; we mean *real* details about actual problems, specific causes of the problems, the personal or business impact of the problems, and the capabilities required to solve the problems or meet the needs—in a measurable way. On business Web sites, we often encounter a section called "Solutions"; however, most of the solutions content is just repackaged product- or service-related jargon. In Part Two of this book, we will discuss these pseudo-solutions in greater detail.

Most "solutions" are often little more than repackaged product- or service-related minutiae and jargon.

In addition, there is often a common, and we believe flawed, assumption that customers understand the extent to which certain types of products and services actually address their critical business issues—another part of the assumptive mindset. In many relatively mature markets, however, offerings have become so complex that companies hire *external* experts to help them select the "best" solution.

Think of the irony of this situation. We hire experts from *outside* of our own companies to help us understand how products will meet *our* needs. What does this illustrate about how easy it is to trace our way from actual problems we are experiencing to the product features and functions? A classic case in point is the customer relationship management (CRM) marketplace. By the late 1990s, industry research indicated that typical enterprise customers utilized approximately 40 percent of existing functionality in the CRM products they purchased. In essence, products had become so overengineered over time that the majority of customers weren't able to apply significant portions of functionality effectively.

What customers *do* understand is what they are *experiencing*; they relate to the symptoms and impact of the problems and needs they have. But in spite of the solutions clamor, most companies are still very much focused on the superiority of what *they* make or do, not on what their customers are experiencing in the form of problems and needs. In fast-growing, demand-rich markets it may be adequate to have a "build it and they will come" mindset, but that is typically a short-lived scenario. As markets mature and competition intensifies, companies will have a compelling edge if they develop the ability to "connect" *first* to the customer problem experience, and then to provide a clear linkage to how their capabilities address the problem.

FOCUSING ON THE CUSTOMER PROBLEM

This approach of focusing on the customer problem has been how many companies have attempted to retool their sales organizations—by teaching them to provide the problem-to-solution linkage. But if there is one overarching theme of this book, it is this: Connecting effectively with real customer problems and needs won't happen consistently by simply training the sales force on how to be more consultative—it's the corporate DNA that will ultimately either drive or suppress sustainable change.

We are convinced there is something almost *jolting* that has to take place in organizations—something that is both galvanizing and meaningful in terms of a real mindset change. To some extent, we're talking about inverting the typical corporate thought process by framing the company's identity and purpose around client problems and needs, not around its products and services. Like the riptide example, you can't just swim harder in the same direction and survive.

To create an authentic solution-centric organization, executives must look past the sales department into the inner workings and DNA of the entire organization.

In addition to a mindset change, we're equally focused on *rigor*. We believe it is the combination of a mindset change and the adoption of rigor that is essential for making a sustainable transformation. But it's also critical to realize rigor itself can be misapplied and misunderstood—many companies are highly rigorous in their support of *product-centric* strategy, tactics, and execution. What we're talking about are *specific* forms of rigor that systemically support an organization-wide problem-solving orientation.

THE SOLUTIONS BANDWAGON

Success breeds competition, period.
If you are successful, you will be imitated.

Companies must *become solutions providers as a means to decommoditize their offerings and provide a clearer linkage to customer value.*

SOLUTIONS ARE IN VOGUE

Who doesn't want to be perceived as a provider of solutions? The race is on. In fact, it is hard to imagine a business concept more prevalent in today's marketplace than *solutions*. While the concept of solutions as an offering originated primarily in business-to-business markets, today the term *solution* is everywhere you turn. There are transportation solutions for drivers, footwear solutions for every conceivable form of sport or exercise, eyewear solutions for the visually impaired, cooking solutions for the domestically challenged, travel solutions for the vacationer, and the list goes on ad infinitum. In fact, virtually every industry or market is touting some form of solution, ranging from the simplest commodity to the most complex industrial or engineered product or service.

Not only do companies want their offerings to be perceived as solutions, companies themselves desire to be perceived in a different light—as a provider of solutions versus the maker of products or provider of services. For example, on January 18, 2005, *USA Today* vividly illustrated this trend by citing initiatives by Intel, HP, Oracle, and SAP that will focus on new market approaches that are solution-focused.

Selling solutions has never been more ubiquitous in the popular press.

In fact, practically everywhere you turn the new mandate to position and "sell" solutions is top-of-mind in research and sales-related publications. Some recent examples include the following:

- "Banks want to position themselves as solution providers…." (First Research)
- "Executives will also generate this productivity—and gain a competitive edge by engaging in more aggressive selling of solutions, not just products and services." (Sales & Marketing Management)
- "Senior-most executives, not just sales, must make solution selling the company's mission if they are to be successful and profitable." (IDC)

In addition, the trend has woven its way into a number of familiar corporate conversations. In all probability, you've heard one or more of the following directives in your company in the past several years.

"Our sales organization needs to be more consultative."

"We need to attain the status of 'trusted advisor' with our customers."

"We need to be perceived as providers of a total customer solution."

But what is driving this near-universal phenomenon? Why are companies that have a legacy of providing perfectly good products and services so caught up in the solutions movement? Like many trends, there is not a single answer to the question but rather multiple, related factors that are driving corporate behaviors. Some of them are:

- The shift from a demand-rich to a demand-poor environment
- Globalization and commoditization
- The daunting challenge of sustained growth
- The potential upside from a revenue and profitability perspective

FACTOR 1: THE SHIFT FROM A DEMAND-RICH TO A DEMAND-POOR ENVIRONMENT

Before assuming your revenue growth problem is primarily a sales organization issue, it's important to recognize how the overall selling environment has evolved in the past five to six years. For the better part of two decades prior to the year 2000, many industries were operating in a *demand-rich* environment. For example, the adoption of enterprise resource planning (ERP) by thousands of companies and including fears over the Y2K challenge created a demand-rich environment for ERP and related technologies. ERP sales organizations focused on effectively managing the pipeline of opportunities that were being generated during this period of widespread adoption. In this environment, we saw the expansion of *opportunity (funnel) management* and *strategic account management* methodologies. That is, most of the sales management and methodology focus was "in the funnel," as illustrated in the bottom half of Figure 2.1.

By contrast, in the post-2000 economic environment, we have witnessed the end of momentum buying in many industries and a general economic slowdown. Today, many of the companies are concerned with the decrease in qualified opportunities they are experiencing. This scenario has also been validated by industry research as well—in recent studies by CSO Insights and Sirius

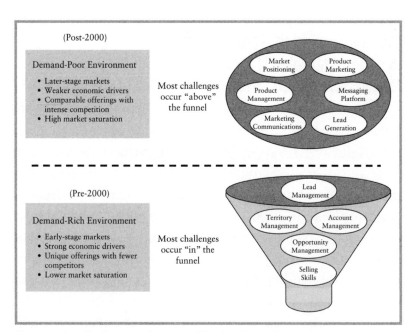

Figure 2.1 Challenges above and in the Funnel

Decisions, lead generation has surfaced as a critical issue in overall top-line effectiveness. In fact, CSO Insights has dubbed 2006 "the year of the lead."

In addition, the advent of the Internet has increased buyer literacy dramatically in the past decade. Buyers now have much more extensive and cheaper access to information, so their ability to research product and service alternatives and to negotiate with potential suppliers has increased dramatically. In such situations, pre-seeding buyers early on with the right market positioning messages, and following up with accurate and timely marketing communications, becomes much more important so that buyers are "connecting" with actual problems that your organization solves long before they enter sales discussions.

This demand-poor backdrop tends to amplify many of the above-the-funnel factors, as illustrated in the upper half of Figure 2.1. These factors are less critical in demand-rich periods when the flow of potential opportunities is more than adequate. To effectively sell in today's demand-poor environment, however, companies are being forced to address a new set of challenges—just to get the *opportunity* to participate. Some of these challenges include the following factors:

- The information avalanche is creating significantly more choices and options for providers and their offerings—with the explosion of media outlets, formats, and content, buyer audiences are far more fragmented these days, and buyers are overwhelmed with messages from multiple sources. A salesperson's messages must be more finely targeted, more relevant, and unusually compelling to even build awareness, let alone to stimulate trial or purchase decisions.

- With much more rapid copying of innovative products' features and functions, there is often less perceived differentiation between similar products in many categories. Higher levels of industry-specific literacy are required to connect with potential buyer decision makers.

- The ability to create *urgency* is increasingly critical; these days, more and more opportunities end in no decision because purchasing decisions are being scrutinized much more closely from a value and return-on-investment (ROI) perspective. Salespeople need to understand the buying organization's decision dynamics to create the compelling reason to act now.

- Buying committee size has increased significantly in the past five years, making personal relationships much less leveragable. Often salespeople need to create effective webs of interrelated relationships to support the case for a purchase decision.

The proliferation of information and the commoditization of products and services are two factors that have made it increasingly difficult for companies to cut through the noise.

In order to successfully address the challenges of competing in such a demand-poor selling environment, companies are compelled to address a broader set of value questions, just to earn the *right* to engage with prospects. These include:

Positioning. How are we positioned in this demand-poor marketplace, and what is the actual customer perception of what we offer?

Messaging. Are our key marketing messages all about us and our offerings, or are they about the problems and needs our potential customers are experiencing?

Preference. Are we caught up in our own engineering brilliance, or do we have a legitimate, defensible platform for differentiation and a relevant story that matters to the customer?

Value defensibility. Are we actually creating products and services that have *defensible* value at the point of sale?

Communications. Does the content of our marketing communications both speak the customer's language in terms of problems and issues, and consistently parallel actual sales conversations?

Demand generation. Do our demand generation vehicles focus on customers' pressing problems and needs, or do they focus on our products' features and functions and their inherent superiority?

Again, the answers to all these questions have a material impact on simply *earning* the right to engage with prospective customers in a demand-poor environment. The relevance to the solutions trend is straightforward—companies are striving to repackage themselves as providers of solutions to elevate their perception in the marketplace. They are hoping to "cut through the noise" in a more relevant and compelling way with potential buyers. By minting new terms, marketers attempt to create a perception of innovation.

FACTOR 2: GLOBALIZATION AND COMMODITIZATION

While getting the opportunity to compete is increasingly demanding, the intensification of competition itself is seen as the most significant challenge in driving sustained growth by senior executives. In fact, in a recent global survey, 80 percent of CEOs see increased competition as the most significant market factor impacting their companies. As Morningstar so aptly commented recently,

> Success breeds competition as surely as night follows day.

It almost goes without saying; if you are successful, you *will* be imitated. As a result, the ability to create and sustain defensible differentiation becomes progressively more difficult in virtually all markets, which often leads to a commodity perception—accompanied by declining revenue growth and margin erosion. We call this decline the "path to commoditization," as illustrated in Figure 2.2.

This path is a familiar scenario with almost any company that has competed in a market that has moved from its fast growth stages though maturity.

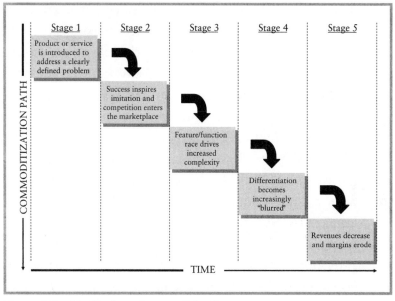

Figure 2.2 The Path to Commoditization

Stage 1: A product or service is introduced to address a clearly defined problem. An example of this is contact management in the early 1990s. The problem was simple: Salespeople were keeping valuable customer information in scattered manual systems. In many cases, follow-up actions were falling through the cracks. When salespeople left the company, the customer database left with them. The solution was simple in concept: an automated tool to allow salespeople to keep accurate, timely contact records for customers and prospects.

Stage 2: Success inspires competition. As soon as one or more companies begin to experience success, competitors begin to arrive. By the mid-1990s, contact management had a new name, sales force automation (SFA), and more than 500 sales automation vendors had arrived in the marketplace. Industry analysts and "gurus" were rapidly building evaluation models for the requisite features and functions of sales force automation.

Stage 3: The feature/function race. At this stage, the "more is better" mindset sets in and competitive paranoia arrives in full force. Highly capitalized vendors begin to enter the marketplace. By the mid to late 1990s, SFA became *CRM* (customer relationship management). Consulting firms and industry analysts built entire practices around CRM. Armies of consultants helped their clients select and install; analysts offered sophisticated methodologies that actually provided a mathematical score for evaluating competing CRM products. The implication was clear—the higher the score, the better the product, and the actual business value of features became sublimated to feature/function "weight."

Stage 4: Differentiation blur sets in. In this stage, products have acquired so many comparable features and functions that it is difficult for customers to differentiate between offerings. In addition, the ability to ascertain the relative business value of competing offerings becomes daunting—companies resort to external experts and opinions in order to make a selection. By the late 1990s, industry studies indicated that almost 60 percent of CRM functionality was largely unused in corporate implementations. Two-thirds of CRM implementations were unable to demonstrate measurable ROI, and momentum buying was replaced by skepticism and caution.

Stage 5: Sales revenue and margin growth decline. Steep discounting becomes the norm for most sales opportunities at this stage, and list price is not taken seriously by buyers. By the early 2000s, a major industry consolidation had taken place. Today, a handful of the original CRM vendors remains—some have been acquired, but many simply faded out of the marketplace.

Recap of the Five Stages to Commoditization

1. A product is brought to market that satisfies an unfilled need.
2. Competitors enter the market.
3. The feature/function race goes into high gear.
4. Differentiation blur sets in.
5. Sales revenue and operating margins decline.

Globalization Accelerates Commoditization

While most viable markets ultimately follow a predictable maturity cycle, what is especially problematic in today's markets is the *pace* at which these cycles are beginning to occur. A compounding factor in the path to commoditization is the rapid emergence of the global economy, which has accelerated the "imitation" factor significantly. Not only can your successful idea be copied, it can be copied quickly and probably far less expensively by hundreds of potential low-cost competitors who previously were not even on the competitive radar screen. The abundance and free flow of instantaneous information is compressing the "advantage cycle" much more quickly than ever thought possible. And the competitive China price for a product, or the India price for an internal function such as customer service, changes a company's economics in ways that simply were not imaginable 5, let alone 10 to 15, years ago.

As a result, it's not just the simple commodity products that are under siege—complex *products and services* are shifting to lower-cost, global providers at a rapid pace. As *BusinessWeek* recently noted:

What is unfolding is the commoditization of knowledge. We have seen global forces undermine autos, electronics, and other manufacturing, but the Knowledge Economy was expected to last forever and play to America's strengths: great universities, terrific labs, smart immigrants, an entrepreneurial business culture. Oops. It turns out there are a growing number of really smart engineers and scientists "out there," too. They've learned to make assembly lines run efficiently, whether they turn out cars or code, refrigerators, or legal briefs.

As a result of this intense competitive scenario, companies have to *really* become solutions providers as a means to decommoditize their offerings and provide a clearer linkage to customer value.

FACTOR 3: THE DAUNTING CHALLENGE OF SUSTAINED GROWTH

Another key force driving the movement to solutions is the near-universal challenge of sustained revenue growth experienced by global corporations. A recent global study (2005) by IBM indicates that an overwhelming number of CEOs (83 percent) around the world are now more focused on growing revenue than slashing costs and want to be more flexible to keep up with changing customer needs.

In short, growing revenues is job number one in nearly every company. Contraction is not a viable long-term strategy, and "acquiring" your way to growth has resulted in mixed, and in some cases disastrous, consequences for some of the world's best-known companies. While the goal of top-line growth may be taking on elevated significance, the challenge of sustaining growth at acceptable levels has proven daunting for the large majority of companies—from 1997 to the present time, the corporations that comprise the Dow Jones Industrial Average have struggled to grow at a collective rate of more than 5 percent, with a mere after-tax profit hovering near 0.5 percent. Recently, Morningstar underscored the extent to which profitable growth is limited to a small minority of companies with the following comment:

We're big fans of companies that generate economic profits, but we're *skeptical* of the ability for many firms to do so for very long. After all, *success attracts competition* as surely as night follows day, which is why *barely 10%* of our 1,400-plus stock-coverage universe earns a wide economic-moat designation.

In other words, if you are an investor placing bets on the consistent profitable growth prospects of corporations, beware. The struggle to grow has also been compellingly documented in a number of recent business books, most notably Michael Treacy's *Double Digit Growth* (published by Portfolio, 2003), in which the author provides a wealth of statistical and anecdotal evidence about the growth challenges experienced by many of the world's best-known companies. While there is no need to revisit this material here, the degree to which the growth problem exists is summarized rather stridently by Treacy as follows:

The truth is that big chunks of Corporate America, along with their counterparts in Asia and Europe, have fallen victim to no growth paralysis.

While this is a rather harsh indictment, it is supported by an extensive body of facts and research. In addition, studies conducted by Bain & Company have revealed compelling findings that further underscore the difficulties that companies face from a sustained growth perspective. Bain evaluated the performance of 2,000 companies over a 10-year period (1987–1997) to understand trends in profitable growth. Over the 10-year period, only 14 percent of the companies were able to maintain a 5.5 percent annual income growth (and corresponding shareholder growth). Note that this was during a relatively robust economic period. In addition, they commented:

> Many firms find these targets—5.5% revenue and net income growth and positive shareholder value creation—achievable for short periods of time, but nearly all stumble sooner or later (and mostly sooner). Fewer than 40% were able to sustain this performance on average for two years, fewer than 20% did it for four years, and only 14% succeeded for more than five years.

In short, sustained and profitable growth has emerged as the universal challenge confronting most businesses today, and companies are hungry for ideas to address this challenge.

Value Invisibility

There are many hypotheses, from strategic to tactical, about how to effectively drive growth. But in simplest terms, the inability to grow means that not enough buyers are choosing your offerings at a profitable price point. Either they aren't buying at all, are opting for an alternative, or are not willing to concede to a price point that is necessary for you to sustain acceptable profitability. While there are many possible causal factors for stagnant or declining growth, in our experience with most companies, failure to grow is typically synonymous with failure to sell. That is, companies genuinely believe their offerings provide real value to customers, but for some reason, not enough buyers are connecting with that value proposition. We call this the "value invisibility" problem. In Parts Three and Four of this book, we explore the systemic drivers of this problem in great detail.

Don't automatically assume that customers "get" your value proposition.

If you don't think the *internal* perception of value to customers is pervasive in your organization, try this simple experiment. Take an informal survey of key executives in your company and ask the following question: "Do the offerings of our company consistently provide legitimate, defensible value to our customers?" What are the probabilities of getting a "no" response to this question? In fact, the mere existence of your customer base means hundreds, if not thousands, of customers have, at some point in time, been willing to part with their money to buy your offerings. So in many cases, flat or declining growth is often distilled into one fairly simple problem.

There is a fundamental disconnect between the internal perception of the value of your offerings and the customer's perception of that value.

For some reason, not enough prospective customers are aware of the value you offer, or they aren't sufficiently convinced of that value to cause a purchase decision. It's that simple.

This is where the solutions movement comes into play, because the term *solution* has a broader connotation than *product* or *service*. Companies increasingly believe they can enhance the perception of value with customers by positioning themselves as providers of solutions, instead of discrete products and services. In Part Two, we will explore in greater detail the various ways in which companies are attempting to be perceived as providers of solutions to drive sales revenue and profitability growth.

FACTOR 4: THE POTENTIAL UPSIDE FROM A REVENUE AND PROFITABILITY PERSPECTIVE

While we may not be able to name a model company that meets all our criteria for being solution-centric, some companies have fared better than others in their attempts to implement a solutions strategy. Some are part way on the journey, and some are committed to the successful transformation from selling products to selling solutions. Consider UPS, for example. In October 2003, John Beystehner, UPS's senior vice president of worldwide sales and marketing, announced:

> But beyond a focus on products, our entire sales function now rests on a new "solutions selling" model, rather than on products and services. In

essence, we're teaching our salespeople to be comfortable asking big questions in corner offices. They're asking business leaders, "What are your business objectives?" and, "What are you trying to accomplish?" rather than, "How many packages do you ship?"

What's drawing a huge company like UPS to make such a transformation? Research across multiple industries in 2003 by McKinsey & Company indicated that accomplishing the transition is challenging—a full 75 percent of companies who *say* they provide solutions don't seem to be realizing a significant increase in return on sales. However, the small percentage of companies that are beginning to "crack the code" are experiencing gains of an extra 3 to 7 percent return on sales from improved margins, longer and more lucrative contracts and relationships, and access to markets they had previously been unable to penetrate. And with the right approach, the return can likely be even higher—the promise of which is motivating many companies to pursue a solutions approach to key markets. Our experiences over the past 15 years support McKinsey's suggestion that a solutions salesperson may be able to earn even higher premiums than the 3 to 7 percent incremental return on sales reported. But here is the caveat— consistently attaining these levels of improvement requires significantly more than simply training or retooling the sales force.

There's More to Selling Solutions Than Salespeople

McKinsey's winners understood that "selling" a solution is truly different from simply offering a revised bundle of pre-existing products and services. They know that solutions need to be conceived, developed, sold, priced, and delivered differently from a simple amalgam of their components. In other words, winning at selling solutions is not an *incremental* undertaking. You can't just add on another component and adjust pricing models to deliver a higher-margin offering. That's not a real solution—it's simply an expanded bundle that we refer to as a "pseudo-solution" in Part Two of this book.

Selling solutions is not an incremental undertaking—that's a pseudo-solution.

Instead, in a real solution, the measurable value of the integrated whole must be greater than the sum of the parts from the customer's perspective, as increasingly informed customers will pay only for value perceived and ultimately delivered. There can be no "value invisibility" gap. The heart of each successful solution, McKinsey found, is a special combination of detailed customer understanding, the supplier's proprietary technical knowledge, and customization and integration of multiple components into something unique that does a superior job of addressing a customer's most pressing *problems*.

The value received, or *outcome*, is visible to customers and can be articulated clearly by salespeople, so winners can earn measurable premiums that customers believe are well-deserved. The winners take a problem-solving view in numerous ways before, during, and after each solutions selling transaction—through intensive efforts and investment to understand specific problems, their causes, and their impact on the world of the customer. In addition, the key to scaling success in selling solutions is finding sizable customer segments that share similar "problem domains," and aligning with selling channels that can effectively represent the value of those solutions to potential buyers.

Transitioning from selling products or services to selling legitimate solutions, and consistently earning that value premium for doing so, requires a different approach to multiple facets of the overall business model, especially marketing and sales. Let's look at UPS's experience again. To a large extent, the marketplace saw the company as a package delivery vendor. UPS sold to lower-level buyers, often in the mail room or equivalent areas, and rarely to senior corporate executives.

Launching UPS's solutions-oriented offerings successfully in the marketplace required multiple change initiatives within sales and marketing, and as one might expect, changes in other business units, as follows:

- Evolution of a *new corporate mission*, to integrate the flow of goods, information, and funds, summarized as "synchronized commerce"
- Detailed *market research* to examine awareness, perception, and value of the UPS brand and its offerings, across major segments

- The largest *rebranding* initiative in business history as of 2003, including 40,000 employee briefing sessions for UPS's 360,000 employees around the world
- *Development and launch* of a synchronized commerce solution for the midmarket customer segment, to showcase the value the company can deliver through solutions combining the flow of goods, information, and funds
- Launch of a *parallel direct sales campaign* to extend beyond traditional purchasers of package delivery products and services toward the corner office—the CFO or controller who might buy asset-based lending from UPS
- *Integrated use of mass marketing*, including direct mail and telesales, to the target audience
- *Integration of customer service capabilities* to support the new offering
- Improved *feedback from sales to marketing*, and vice versa, to ensure tighter alignment between functions going forward
- Improved *sales training* to equip the sales force with the right knowledge, frameworks, and tools to sell solutions in place of products and services
- *Aligning measurements* to create shared sales goals across all sales groups
- *Aligning compensation* packages to support the new solution selling approach
- *Reassigning organizations* and ensuring the right cross-organization linkages to conduct, reward, and deliver on integrated solutions sales

While it may be too early to judge the long-term impact of these initiatives for UPS, recent financial results in early 2005 are far from discouraging, indicated in the following UPS Press Release:

"We had a great start to the year (2005). The first quarter set the pace for UPS to generate earnings in 2005 at the higher end of our historical range," said Scott Davis, UPS's chief financial officer. "We grew our international operating profit by more than 25%, and we did a very good job of managing our costs. Our cost initiatives are taking hold, and we are benefiting from the deployment of package flow technology in the U.S. operation. There is strong momentum throughout all three business units."

International package revenue increased 13% to $1.84 billion. Operating profit climbed 25.6% to $348 million. Asia export volume increased 36% with export volume doubling out of China. Operating margin increased 190 basis points to 18.9%. U.S. domestic package revenue grew 2.8% during the period to $6.8 billion. Operating profit rose 12.7% to $1.03 billion and operating margin was 15.1%. Average daily volume in the U.S. grew 0.1% for the quarter. Yields remained strong, with an increase in revenue per piece of 2.6% for all U.S. domestic products.

Revenue for the supply chain *solutions segment* increased 86% to $1.23 billion with the addition of Menlo Worldwide Forwarding. Freight services and logistics accounted for $1.12 billion of that total. Revenue growth for the segment was on track and hit its target for the quarter. Profitability was reduced by the integration of Menlo.

"We are confident we've laid the foundation to accelerate volume growth in the U.S. going forward," added Davis. "Our efforts to better sell to mid-sized customers are gaining traction, and we made good strides in connecting more customers to UPS through electronic shipping systems."

Creating a solution-centric enterprise requires a number of significant change initiatives.

While we're not suggesting that every company underwrite the same level of change as UPS at the outset, this example provides an excellent illustration of the range of key tasks facing any company choosing to make such a transformation. While this book maintains a principal focus on the revenue engine (marketing and sales), in Part Four, we discuss some of the broader organizational implications of making the transformation to solution-centricity.

COMMON REACTIONS TO PERFORMANCE PROBLEMS

In some cases, there is a definite sales organization problem, but the danger is in assuming that addressing necessary change in the sales organization will be the singular "lever" that will restore sustainable sales growth.

Companies that view sales effectiveness as the broader, systemic alignment of both marketing and sales organizations are beginning to see some measurable signs of improvement.

UNIVERSAL PROBLEMS

Earlier we posed the question, "What often happens in companies when revenue growth declines?" After being exposed to hundreds of companies in this situation for the past 15 years, we can answer that in an overwhelming majority of cases, the most common hypothesis is that there is a *sales* problem. In part, this is because there is typically a very observable correlation to sales operations metrics. That is, lower revenue is often accompanied by lower win rates, lower quota attainment, steeper discounting, etc. Also, as we mentioned earlier, when companies have been successful in the past at creating products and services customers will buy, they assume that the breakdown must be taking place during the sale. In some cases, there is a definite *sales* organization problem, but the danger is in assuming that addressing necessary change in the sales organization will be the singular "lever" that will restore sustainable sales growth.

To prepare for this book, we cataloged the "symptoms" our clients have typically attributed to their sales performance problems. While this is not intended to be exhaustive, it provides a good representation of what clients typically say they are *experiencing*. These problems manifest themselves as one or more of the following:

- Products and services are increasingly perceived as commodities
- Difficulty positioning value and differentiating offerings
- Difficulty selling complex offerings and winning major opportunities
- Late into opportunities, too frequently reacting to requests for proposal (RFPs)
- Lack of qualified leads in the pipeline
- Wide variations in forecast accuracy
- Inability to stimulate interest or create demand
- Unable to access buying power and sell effectively to executives
- Wide variation in quota attainment
- Lengthy sales cycles and frequent "no decisions"
- Frequent pursuit of unqualified opportunities
- Failure to realize sales potential in major accounts

Companies have responded to these problems in a variety of ways, ranging from strategic sales transformation initiatives through tactical training projects, with a wide range of outcomes. In our recent experience, however, four of the most common reactions to sales revenue growth and margin erosion have been the following:

1. *We must fix (i.e., train) the sales force.* Most companies genuinely believe their products and services

provide legitimate value to customers, but the customers aren't "getting it." That is, the sales organization must not be articulating the real value of offerings effectively to prospects, and, therefore, sales are off. Assuming that the sales problem is "localized," some form of training is arranged for the sales force. In some cases, sales training is entirely appropriate; but there are many other factors involved in revenue performance that often are unattended to, and performance gains are often short-lived.

2. *We need to offer solutions versus products or services.* Because success invites imitation, over time many products are perceived as commodities. Or, as industries mature, products become so complex and feature-rich that "differentiation blur" sets in. As described earlier, with limited defensible differentiation, companies have responded by positioning themselves as solutions providers. In many cases, this simply equates to bundling products with associated services—accompanied with the declaration, "We now provide a total solution for the customer."

3. *We need to fire the sales leader.* Research indicates that in large corporations, the average tenure of the chief sales officer (CSO) is 22 months. In other words, if the sales team isn't winning within two years, it's time to fire the coach. This is the ultimate case of a "localized" view of the problem—a single individual in the corporation is identified as the cause of sales performance problems.

4. *Some combination of 1, 2, and 3.* Often the effort to transition to a solution or value orientation is primarily focused on the sales force. In this case, some form of training is typically sponsored by the sales leader to teach sales professionals how to sell value versus products and services. Again, there often is no change in the underlying offering, the systemic factors that are "upstream" from sales, or the reinforcement vehicles that are critical for sustainable change. In some cases, the sales improvement initiative may also be accompanied by superficial messaging and packaging changes, which we refer to as "pseudo-solutions" and discuss in greater detail in Chapter Four.

In other words, there is a great deal more focus on *perception* and salesperson education than on understanding sales performance problems from a systemic perspective. What is typically absent is a *rigorous* approach across the organization to understand real customer problems, why they exist, how they impact the customer operationally and financially, and what to do about them.

IS THE SITUATION IMPROVING?

With the backdrop of limited growth, intensifying global competition, and a demand-poor environment, are companies striving to overcome their inability to sell enough of their offerings at an acceptable price point? The answer is a resounding yes. First, from an anecdotal perspective, most of the readers of this book have probably experienced multiple sales improvement initiatives in their corporate careers. In fact, IDC reports that the number one investment line item in the sales organization budget is for sales-related training. While a definitive overall investment number is not easy to derive, there are some research estimates that suggest that as much as $5 billion annually is spent on corporate initiatives to improve top-line performance. In addition, Jim Dickie, founder of CSO Insights, indicates that some 300 to 400 firms in the United States are currently providing services to address revenue and sales performance problems. In short, companies are spending, and spending significantly, to address improved sales performance.

Some five billion dollars is spent annually on improvement initiatives.

The question is then, "To what extent are these investments paying off?" While case studies indicate some performance improvements have clearly taken place, industry studies and broad economic outcomes strongly suggest many companies have not advanced significantly at positioning value consistently with customers. At the macro level, relatively few industry sectors have been growing much faster or more profitably than the broad economy—recall the prior comments from Morningstar about the 1,400 companies that it covers, Bain's study on profitable growth, and the "growth crisis" described in great detail in Michael Treacy's *Double Digit Growth*. Other targeted studies tend to support the thesis that most companies are making, at best, marginal improvements in marketing and selling high-value solutions in their respective markets. Consider the following:

1. Many, perhaps most, salespeople do not know how to position the value of their offerings properly. A study attributed to the American Marketing Association reported that as few as *1 in 10 salespeople know how to position value and use messages correctly and consistently*. If true, such a figure means that companies simply remain inept at teaching salespeople how to effectively position defensible value with customers.

2. The American Marketing Association's Customer Message Management Forum estimates that *up to 90 percent of marketing tools and sales support materials never get used in the field*. And *BtoB* magazine reported *70 percent of companies grade their marketing messaging and sales support functions as D or F* on a scale from A to F. Numerous industry analysts have assessed similar questions—consider the massive efforts to determine the ROI (return on investment) on marketing expenditures, as one example, or the need for marketing accountability. While the "over 90 percent" level appears surprisingly, and perhaps even atrociously, high, it is not intuitively wrong. Often marketing remains seriously disconnected from sales, and marketing materials are fun-

damentally not aligned with what a company's sales force needs.

3. As we mentioned earlier, CSO Insights' annual "State of the Marketplace Review" reported in 2004 that "51% of sales representatives were under quota." Although in 2005 the under-quota proportion had dropped to 42 percent, much of that improvement is attributed to salespeople simply working longer and harder to make their numbers, which is difficult to sustain consistently for extended periods. To quote CSO Insights in 2005: "We are still taking too long to get new reps up to speed, are still seeing low win rates, and reps are continuing to use discounts to close business far too often." Furthermore, CSO Insights' data reveals that in both 2004 and 2005, only 45 percent of salespeople are rated Very Good or World Class in their ability to deliver consistent messages to prospects—the rest are Dismal, Poor, or simply Average. And in 2005 the ability to effectively present offering *benefits* (value) actually fell, despite a continuing trend away from selling products and toward selling solutions.

4. We know that *sales training alone does not equip salespeople to position value well.* A survey of more than 6,000 sales professionals conducted by Sales Performance International in 2003 showed that the half-life of typical training events is about five weeks in the absence of consistent reinforcement. In fact, without specific, ongoing reinforcement for the training experience, 86 percent of what is learned is not

retained within three months. It should be no surprise, then, that CSO Insights discovered such low quota attainment. And it should also be no wonder that salespeople have difficulty positioning value effectively with customers—most companies don't do a good enough job of helping salespeople learn, retain, and apply the lessons they would like, and expect, them to learn about how to sell discrete products and services, much less how to sell complex solutions.

All in all, in spite of significant investments in improvement, it is far from evident whether fundamental metrics of sales performance are improving significantly on a *sustainable* basis and whether companies are becoming more adept at positioning their offerings with their customers. Yet some rays of light seem to be emerging. A 2004 study by Aberdeen stated that "sales effectiveness initiatives can and do have a positive impact on the business." Of particular interest were the following observations:

> Aberdeen Group discovered a very strong and mostly unnoticed correlation between the degree of collaboration within a company and the effectiveness of that company's sales force. This finding supports the idea that selling is increasingly becoming a *team* rather than individual activity. Collaboration is particularly critical between the *sales and marketing* departments of organizations. Again, Aberdeen discovered that companies that

had strong collaboration between the two functions had higher sales effectiveness, and this was especially true where there were *structured* processes and systems in place to support this collaboration.

In other words, companies that attempt to view sales effectiveness as the broader, systemic alignment of both marketing and sales organizations are beginning to see some measurable signs of improvement. Parts Two and Three of this book explore why companies struggle with the transition to selling solutions, and how to understand and address the systemic barriers to sustained improvement.

SOLUTION-CENTRIC CONCEPTS AND PRINCIPLES

THE EMERGENCE OF PSEUDO-SOLUTIONS

As products and services become more complex, the ability for customers to trace their way from problems to the appropriate solution components becomes increasingly daunting.

An analysis of aspiring solution providers reveals a number of positioning maneuvers that attempt to convey a greater value message to potential buyers. These are superficial initiatives that we call pseudo-solutions, *which are largely terminology and packaging manipulations.*

YOUR DNA IS STILL PRODUCT-CENTRIC

Not so, you say. It's hard to find a company today that doesn't claim to provide solutions to their customers. In fact, most companies' products and services address *some* of the problems and needs of their customers, or they would fail to exist. What we're really talking about is a matter of degree. The question isn't whether your offerings solve problems and address real needs—it's the *extent* to which your organization is *aligned* to successfully and consistently address those customer problems and needs better than your competitors. It isn't just about listening to customers. It isn't just about how you conduct the sales conversation. It isn't just about how you communicate in the marketplace. It isn't just about how you set product or service priorities. It's about whether *all* these things are driven from a common frame of reference.

Wait a minute, though—this is starting to sound rather complicated. If the enemy of change is complexity, addressing all these issues simultaneously sounds overwhelming, doesn't it? Weren't we talking earlier about a *finite* number of manageable transformation points? In fact, we still are. In this section of the book, we will discuss *four* fundamental transformations that are integral to transitioning from being product-centric to solution-centric. But before we present these transformation ideas, we need to first consider and confront the extent to which we still live in a highly product-centric world.

To explore this hypothesis on our own, we picked 200 business-to-business (B2B) companies from the Global 2000 that claim to offer some form of a solution on their Web sites. The Global 2000 is a list compiled by Forbes (www.forbes.com) that shows the biggest companies as measured by a composite ranking of sales, profits, assets, and market value. While the corporate Web site is not the only form of marketing communication, these days it tends to be the primary "window to the world" for most companies. We evaluated the solutions areas of each site against the following criteria:

1. How clearly does the solutions area of the site capture the problem state facing the customer? That is, what specific problems, needs, and challenges is the customer experiencing?

2. Are the causal factors or drivers for these problems identified clearly? What internal and external forces are actually creating the existing problem state?

3. Is the business impact, from both an operational and financial perspective, clearly linked to the causal factors? To what extent do specific problems have a negative impact on the overall business? What are the consequences of not addressing the problem or need—or what are the consequences of delay?

4. What capabilities are required to address the actual *causes* of the problem state? What does success look like?

5. How does the solution provide the needed capabilities to address the causes of the problem state?

After reviewing the selected Web sites, we summarized our results in the table shown in Figure 4.1.

While these findings aren't the ultimate litmus test for solution-centricity, they provide a good overall indicator as to how many companies think about what it means to offer solutions. We're reasonably confident that if we were to explore another 100, 500, or 1,000 Web sites, we would see a similar pattern, and the observed pattern tends to suggest the following:

	None	Limited Specifics	Moderate Specific	Highly Specific
(1) Articulation of problem state	3%	48%	41%	1%
(2) Linkage of causal factors	30%	55%	14%	1%
(3) Capabilities required to address causes	27%	46%	23%	4%
(4) Operational and financial impact linkages	34%	49%	16%	3%
(5) Solution linkage to address causes	37%	44%	16%	3%

Figure 4.1   Web Site Solution-Messaging Evaluation Report

- Most companies that claim to sell solutions continue to define who they are by what *products* they make or provide—more than half of the companies evaluated offered few specifics about what *problems* they actually solve, and only 1 percent of companies did an exceptional job of providing problem specifics.
- Most companies assume buyers understand *why* they are experiencing their problems and what their needs are—85 percent of sites offered very little to educate buyers about the causes of their problems.
- Very few companies provide specific linkages between problems their customers are experiencing and the operational and financial impact of those problems—more than 80 percent of companies fail to provide material specifics about these linkages.
- Companies do a reasonably good job of communicating what *they* provide in the way of capabilities, but again, the clear linkage between problems, their causes, and those capabilities is nearly nonexistent—more than 80 percent of companies fail to create coherent linkages between the capabilities of their offerings and problems.

In other words, it is incumbent on customers to reverse-engineer their way from the "solutions" that are being provided to an understanding of how these so-called solutions address their actual business problems. As products and services become more complex, the ability for customers to trace their way from problems they are experiencing to the appropriate solution components becomes

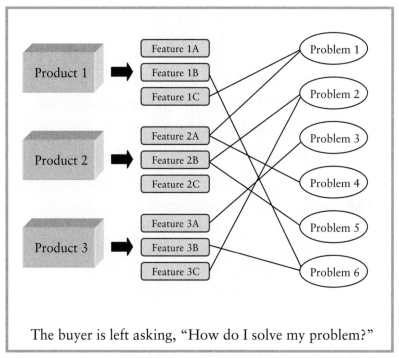

The buyer is left asking, "How do I solve my problem?"

Figure 4.2 Problem-Solution Traceability Challenge

increasingly daunting. They can't figure out which features of which products will help them resolve the set of problems they face. This "problem-solution traceability" challenge, illustrated in Figure 4.2, is why companies often turn to external experts to help them unravel the feature/function relevance of the potential solution.

Some may argue that a corporate Web site itself is not sufficient to explore this level of problem analysis and that other forms of collateral, such as white papers or data sheets, may delve deeper into specific problems and challenges that solutions address. While this may be true in part, we pose the simple question, "Why is the inventory of problems and challenges typically sublimated several layers deep in the story, if it is addressed at all?"

Most corporate communications (e.g., on Web sites) are not consultative in nature and do little to address authentic solutions.

The reason we pose this question is that if we are asking the sales force to be more consultative and to become better at diagnosing customer problems and needs, why are other forms of corporate communications exempt from the same type of conversations?

THE PRODUCT-SOLUTION CLASH

A phenomenon that we observed with increasing frequency is something we have termed the *product-solution clash*. Most of the emphasis around the solutions topic today remains highly focused on *selling* solutions. As we discussed earlier, this is often an expected, simplistic reaction to growth challenges—readily blaming growth problems on the sales organization.

In essence, the corporate DNA remains largely product-centric while the sales organization is expected to transform to selling solutions. Substantial investments are made to retool the sales organization, but very little consideration is given to upstream factors that can significantly contribute to sales interaction effectiveness. In addition, the challenge of change management is often significantly underestimated. Not only can improvement initiatives be suboptimal, they can actually be close to being "throwaways." The attempts to fix the sales force can result in a sometimes pronounced collision with other corporate values, priorities, and practices.

In other words, what we have experienced as product-centric DNA can be a major inhibitor to sustained Solution Selling mastery. As we mentioned earlier, we have found that in the absence of formal, systemic reinforcement, the half-life of sales training retention is 30 days; within three months, 86 percent of knowledge can be lost. If the overall mindset and practices of the organization are highly product-centric, the reinforcement can actually be negative. This potential clash is depicted in Figure 4.3.

As the illustration depicts, many of the defining attributes of companies tend to begin aligned with a product

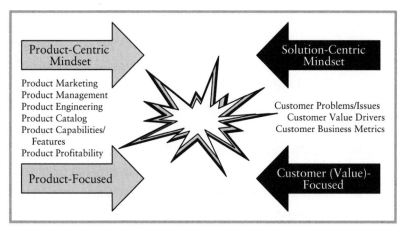

Figure 4.3 The Product-Solution Clash

orientation. Companies are often organized extensively around products or product lines, which tends to place products at the forefront of the corporate mindset. When efforts to transform the sales organization occur in this environment, it can be extremely challenging to make the necessary handoffs and translations between sales and the rest of the company.

PSEUDO-SOLUTION MANEUVERS

The desire to be perceived as a provider of solutions has not only resulted in projects to retool the sales organization. An analysis of aspiring solution providers reveals a number of positioning maneuvers that attempt to convey a greater value message to potential buyers. We refer to these mostly superficial initiatives as *pseudo-solutions*, which are largely terminology and packaging manipulations that include the following:

- *The messaging maneuver.* In many cases, companies simply substitute the term *solution* for *product* or *service*. In other words, they simply adjust their high-level messaging to use solution-oriented terms and phrases with little or no attention paid to the problems customers are experiencing.
- *The bundling maneuver.* When services are required to implement or support a product, they are offered as a "bundle," and this combination of products and

services is labeled a "total solution" for the customer. In technology-related industries, the bundling of products and services into a "package" is probably the most common use of the term *solution*. In other cases, several existing products are bundled to form a "solution" package.

- *The specialization maneuver.* In this case, a basic product is slightly altered to better meet the requirements or appear to meet requirements for a specific industry or constituency and termed a *tailored solution*. This is done to create the perception of specialization for a targeted buyer.

- *The functional maneuver.* A common practice for many organizations is to identify a functional area of a company and then label their offering a "solution" for that area. For example, "we provide a human resource solution" or "we provide a complete telecom management solution."

It's important at this point to note that some of these approaches are reasonable ideas and are not necessarily bad for the customer. Clearly, there are situations where bundling products and services or adapting offerings for vertical requirements helps to address certain customers' problems. Tailoring products and services for specific constituencies or functions can be valuable as well. However, none of these approaches by *necessity* provides a solution for customers, nor do they necessarily have a material impact on a company's sales capabilities.

"Pseudo-solutions" include messaging maneuvers, bundling maneuvers, specialization maneuvers, and functional maneuvers.

In other words, none of these maneuvers by default make it easier for customers to trace their way from specific problems they are experiencing to the corresponding solution components. In addition, they may do very little to address a real problem more effectively in a measurable way. In Chapter Five, we will explore some specific criteria for whether or not an offering qualifies as a legitimate solution.

A recent comment by a senior sales executive we interviewed captured the essence of the problem perfectly:

We can solve so many problems for the organizations we sell to, but we make it extremely hard for the customer to understand what those problems are and how our offerings address them.

We couldn't have said it better. The question to pose within your organization is, "Why make it so hard?" Even if you are selling to esoteric or sophisticated buyers, why assume they are capable of making the problem-solution connection?

FOUR AREAS OF HIGH-LEVEL DIAGNOSIS

Throughout the remainder of this book, we will continue to press on this point: How do we align key aspects of marketing and sales to support what we want to occur when the salesperson engages in dialogue with the customer? A good starting point is to assess, at a high level, the extent to which your organization is currently product-centric versus solution-centric. To help with this exercise, the following pages provide a set of comparative characteristics in four key areas of assessment. As you walk through each section, attempt to honestly consider whether the attributes in the left column or the right column best describe the current state of your organization.

How Do We Think?

Does our organization tend to think of itself as a provider of products and/or services, or as a solver of customer problems? Review Figure 4.4 to assess your organization.

How Do We Communicate?

Does our organization communicate consistently in terms of the problems we solve, as opposed to the products we make and services we offer? Review Figure 4.5 to assess your organization.

How Do We Engage with Customers?

When we engage with customers, do we add value by helping them understand their problems and how we

HOW DO WE THINK?—ASSESSMENT		
Product-Centric	or	Solution-Centric
• Our identity is largely framed by what we make or provide.		• We tend to define ourselves by the customer transformation that occurs when someone does business with us.
• When introducing our company, we tend to focus on what we provide to the marketplace—it's largely about us.		• When introducing our company, we tend to focus on the problems we solve or needs we meet for customers—it's largely about them.
• When we think about designing products and services, we start from what we can already do, and then work to discover other things we can do for customers that they might value.		• We apply a rigorous methodology to understand specific customer problems and needs, their particular causes, their measurable business impact, and how our offerings address them.
• Sometimes we invest in elegant engineering or "cool" ideas without understanding why, where, or how we can make money from them.		• We don't invest in elegant engineering or "cool" ideas without understanding value "defensibility" at the point of sale.
• We think about developing messages in terms of what we can do and products and services we can offer; we think only secondarily (if at all) about customers' problems.		• We ensure that we have a formalized messaging platform that is based on problems and needs that are critical to customers.
• We don't think about enabling customers to determine how, precisely, our products and services can help them address their specific business problems.		• We think hard about enabling customers to trace the linkages between their specific business problems and the capabilities of our solutions.
• It is not always clear why we want to charge as much as we do and why such prices are justified.		• We make sure the business value of our offerings is rigorously defined and highly defensible at the point of sale.
• It is hard to differentiate our offerings from those of our primary competitors.		• We have a well-defined differentiation framework that clearly conveys our proprietary, comparative, and holistic differentiators.

Figure 4.4   How Do We Think?—Assessment

can address them? Review Figure 4.6 to assess your organization.

How Do We Reinforce?

How do we reinforce our thinking, our messages, and our ways of engaging with customers? Do we employ *specific*

HOW DO WE COMMUNICATE?—ASSESSMENT		
Product-Centric	or	Solution-Centric
• Product marketing starts with existing products and services and does not prioritize target segments based on what we can do for them particularly well.		• Product marketing incorporates a formal problem/solution mapping approach extensively in our targeting, solution definition, and prioritization methods.
• Our Web site presents information on all our products and services without explaining how they can be applied to resolve customer problems.		• Our Web site focuses extensively on customer problems, their causes, and business impact versus presenting products and capabilities.
• It is difficult for a prospect to understand the specific problems we can help them address and to trace the effect of our products and services on those problems.		• It is easy for a prospect to identify with specific problems we address and trace the effect of our solutions on those problems.
• We organize our sales collateral around our products and services.		• We organize our sales collateral around business problems and needs in our target markets.
• We launch products and services— our lead generation campaigns focus on features and benefits.		• We launch "solutions to problems"— our lead generation campaigns focus on customer problems and needs.
• Our sales tools are framed around our product or service features and benefits.		• Our sales tools are framed around specific customer problems and needs.

Figure 4.5 How Do We Communicate?—Assessment

management and support systems that demonstrate commitment to being a legitimate provider of solutions? Review Figure 4.7 to assess your organization.

If the majority of your responses tended to fall in the left-hand columns, or you failed to understand terms and concepts in the right-hand columns, then your DNA is still largely product-centric, and efforts to sell solutions may encounter numerous obstacles.

In Chapter Five, we explore, at a conceptual level, four fundamental transformations that lay the groundwork for moving from being product-centric to solution-centric.

HOW DO WE ENGAGE WITH CUSTOMERS?—ASSESSMENT		
Product-Centric	or	Solution-Centric
• Our salespeople know how to present the features and benefits of our products and services.		• Our salespeople can diagnose customers' true business problems and offer well-defined solutions to solve those problems.
• Our salespeople call at low levels in the organization and discuss the features and benefits of our products and services—they steer clear of higher-level contacts and conversations about an organization's broad business problems.		• Salespeople usually call at the right level in the organization and are comfortable having substantive business conversations with C-level executives.
• Salespeople do a poor job of controlling the buying process and often issue proposals before receiving verbal commitments.		• Salespeople do a good job of controlling the buying process and rarely issue proposals without receiving verbal commitments first.
• Salespeople do not position value well and often resort to steep discounts to win opportunities.		• Salespeople are effective in positioning value and rarely discount steeply to win opportunities.
• We have as many undocumented sales processes as we have salespeople.		• The sales process is documented fully and, for the most part, all salespeople use a common process.
• Our sales process is designed around how our salespeople like to sell.		• Our sales process aligns with our customers' buying processes.

Figure 4.6   How Do We Engage with Customers?—Assessment

HOW DO WE REINFORCE?—ASSESSMENT		
Product-Centric	or	Solution-Centric
• We lack any mechanisms to sustain solution-centric skills and practices.		• We have a formal reinforcement plan in place to ensure that solution-centric skills and practices are sustained.
• Our culture is to move on to the next customer immediately after our product has been sold.		• Our culture is to measure how well we addressed a customer's problem well after implementation.
• Our CRM and other technology tools do not support Solution Selling disciplines.		• CRM and other technology tools provide specific support for Solution Selling disciplines.
• Brochures, literature, and electronic information on our products and services are in place to reinforce seller knowledge of offerings.		• Brochures, literature, and electronic information focus extensively on customer problems, causes, and impact to ensure that joint problem diagnosis and vision creation occur between buyers and sellers.
• We provide little, if any, education for key executives and managers to reinforce their solution-centric behaviors.		• We provide regular education for key executives and managers to effectively mentor and reinforce solution-centric behaviors.
• We lack any structured approach to managing change for initiatives like becoming solution-centric.		• A formal, structured approach is in place to continue successful change management.

Figure 4.7 How Do We Reinforce?—Assessment

FOUR FUNDAMENTAL TRANSFORMATIONS

Four key questions can be dissected to determine if you are product-centric versus solution-centric: How do we think? How do we communicate? How do we engage with customers? How do we reinforce?

Your company story shouldn't be about how great your company's offerings are. Instead, it needs to connect the relevance of your firm's existence to the problems and needs of the customer.

MAKING THE TRANSFORMATION TO
A PROBLEM-SOLVING ORGANIZATION

If messaging and packaging manipulations and specialized versions of products are not in and of themselves solutions, what does it mean to provide a real solution? In order to build a foundation for solution-centric concepts, it's important to consider a concise definition of the term *solution* in a business context.

A solution is a mutually agreed-upon answer to a recognized problem that provides measurable improvement (value).

This definition organizes our thinking about what it means to be truly solution-centric. To a large extent, taking Solution Selling concepts to the next level means becoming a problem-solving organization. That doesn't just mean having a list of problems you intend to address; it means "living the problem" and having a real, in-depth understanding of what's really happening in the world of your customers. In addition, it means having coherent linkages between problems and solutions that demonstrate measurable value. In Chapter Four, we presented a brief set of diagnostic questions in four areas that contrast product-centric versus solution-centric characteristics. In the sections that follow, we will delve more deeply into each of these four areas as follows:

1. *How do we think?* This is the mindset question. Do we define ourselves by the problems we solve or the products that we make?
2. *How do we communicate*, internally and externally? Do we align all aspects of marketing execution with a problem-solving orientation?
3. *How do we engage with customers?* Do we apply Solution Selling disciplines effectively across all sales channels—direct and indirect?
4. *How do we reinforce?* Do we provide formal reinforcement vehicles to both support and sustain solution-centric disciplines?

THINK DIFFERENTLY	Define yourself by the problems you solve versus the products you make.
COMMUNICATE DIFFERENTLY	Align all aspects of marketing execution with a well-defined problem/solution framework.
ENGAGE DIFFERENTLY	Apply Solution Selling disciplines across all sales channels (direct and indirect).
REINFORCE DIFFERENTLY	Provide comprehensive support for solution-centric disciplines.

Figure 5.1 Four Fundamental Transformations

These questions set the stage for the four fundamental transformations, at a conceptual level, that are required to become a solution-centric organization.

Transformation 1: Changing How You Think

THINK DIFFERENTLY	Define yourself by the problems you solve versus the products you make.
COMMUNICATE DIFFERENTLY	Align all aspects of marketing execution with a well-defined problem/solution framework.
ENGAGE DIFFERENTLY	Apply Solution Selling disciplines across all sales channels (direct and indirect).
REINFORCE DIFFERENTLY	Provide comprehensive support for solution-centric disciplines.

On the surface, changing how you think as an organization may seem rather abstract and difficult to act on. However, changing one's mindset is a fundamental first step in most transformations whether personal or in the business world. So what do we mean by saying, "Change how you think"? The answer to that question has multiple dimensions, each of which can be translated into meaningful action.

What's the Big Idea? Try this simple experiment. Poll a cross section of key people in your organization and ask the following question: *"What is the fundamental transformation that occurs in customers who choose to do business with us?"* To answer this question typically requires thinking in a before-and-after mode. That is, what is the customer's state before doing business with us, and how do we help to transform the customer's situation to a more desirable state? What do customers really *get* if they choose us?

In extremely large companies this may be difficult; but at a business unit level, it should be possible to capture such a concept. In all likelihood, you will receive a wide variety of responses depending on who you ask in the organization. In our experience, most individuals tend to struggle to answer this question succinctly. The reason for this is that the identity of most companies tends to be synonymous with what they make or provide. That is, they have been steeped for years or decades in defining themselves around the things they make—their products.

What is the fundamental transformation that occurs in customers who choose to do business with us?

Why is this important? Because this mindset has a trickle-down effect. If the essence of your identity is the products you make, it is likely that product-centric practices and behaviors will permeate your organization. Conversely, if you define or frame your organization's identity around a customer outcome or transformation, it can provide a galvanizing cornerstone for solution-centric transformation. We frequently encounter companies building their "best in the world" concepts around *themselves*—not around a customer transformation.

Mohanbir Sawhney, McCormick Tribune Professor of Technology at the Kellogg School of Management, has recently written extensively on the need for strategic and product marketing to think habitually in terms of customer *outcomes*. While this is not an exercise in branding, a few of the world's best-known companies have built exceptional brand equity around a customer outcome, or what the customer receives or attains, as opposed to actual products or services they provide. An example of this is Disney and the concept of "family friendly." Whether it's a movie, a theme park, a cruise, a resort, or a toy, parents can be assured of a critical *outcome*—it's safe and appropriate for all members of the family. Whether this is a brand per se doesn't matter—to parents "it's a Disney movie" is synonymous with "it's okay for the kids."

The first step in changing how you think is to consider thoughtfully the real purpose of your company in the marketplace—in terms of a customer outcome or transformation. Think this through to the point-of-sales execution: How do you want salespeople to represent the purpose of the company when they're face-to-face with customers? What's the big problem, need, or opportunity your organization addresses for its customers? It may be challenging in a B2B environment to capture this concept succinctly, but if you can, it will help to create the right kind of trickle-down effect—one that begins to frame your company's raison d'etre (reason for being) around a customer problem, need, or opportunity.

Do We Really Understand the Problems We Solve?   One of the questions we have been posing recently to clients who are trying to move to selling solutions is, "Where is your *problem* catalog?" As you might expect, most of the time they're not sure what we mean; or they think we really meant *product* catalog. In truth, this is a trick question, because we don't expect anyone to actually have a problem catalog. The question is meant to jolt people out of their traditional way of thinking.

Does your company have a problem catalog?

Recall that over half of the Web sites we reviewed from solution providers had virtually no mention of actual customer problems. So the next part of changing how you think is to create a comprehensive inventory of problems, needs, and opportunities your customers are experiencing. Just having such a list, however, doesn't mean you're finished. Building a rigorous problem understanding requires answering a structured set of questions that provide traceability from problem → causes → negative consequences → solution → positive change. This problem-solution mapping is the precursor to high levels of situational fluency for multiple parts of the organization. In Part Four, we provide an example of a problem-solution mapping.

Are We Really Different? Another key aspect of changing how we think has to do with differentiation, which is often a widely misunderstood concept. Again, poll a cross section of key people in your organization and ask the following question: "What are our top three competitive differentiators?" In all likelihood, you will receive a wide array of responses that will include product features, benefits, company attributes, and organizational platitudes. In an actual project, we once received 37 different responses from a cross-functional survey to identify the top three differentiators. Clearly, there was no unified understanding as to what actually comprises a differentiator. In many cases, this is true because companies often lack a structured framework for defining points of differentiation. In Part Four, we provide a template for creating a structured differentiation model.

Does Our Story Really Matter? Once you've developed a rigorous understanding of the problems that you solve and defensible differentiators, it is possible to build a messaging platform that is relevant and problem-focused. At this point, we need to distill the overall set of problems, needs, and opportunities we address into a concise set of customer-relevant messages. In other words, we may solve a hundred different problems, but those problems need to be aggregated into some key issues.

> Do your marketing messages
> mirror the conversations your
> salespeople have with customers
> and potential customers?

The operative question here is, "Do our marketing messages consistently parallel the conversations we want the sales force to have with customers?" If we want salespeople to have a dialogue with customers on critical business issues, our messaging platform should be largely based on those same issues. In Part Four, we provide examples of a Critical Business Issue (CBI) Menu and Solution Messaging Cards that form the basis for a solution messaging platform.

Are We Targeting the Right Audience? After building a rigorous value framework and messaging platform, it's important to revisit the marketplace and validate our thinking about the target buyer. Do the problems we solve *actually* have significant relevance for the market segments and customer sponsors that we are targeting? Do the capabilities that we provide address specific critical business issues that our target segments are experiencing in a measurable way? This analysis can produce some surprising conclusions. In some cases, this thought process can actually expose new potential market segments because the product-focused "lens" has been replaced by a problem-focused mindset. In Part Four, we discuss key segmentation concepts that are aligned with a problem-oriented lens.

Are We Selling through the Right Channels? A final step in changing how we think is to revisit our use of selling resources. In practice, we have seen companies fundamentally alter their sales channel models after going through a comprehensive problem-solution mapping and segmentation calibration. Why? Because it is possible that products that appear to have synergy since they are in the same product line may present very different selling challenges. In Part Four, we discuss problem-oriented segmentation concepts that can help guide channel decisions.

Summary Changing how we think fundamentally redefines the *conceptual* framework of the organization—the story of who we are, why we exist as a business, and why it matters to customers. In addition, it calibrates that story with the right types of potential buyers and the right selling resources. This aligns us conceptually with solution-centric principles. The next step is to align a key aspect of execution—how we actually *tell* that story.

Transformation 2: Changing How You Communicate

THINK DIFFERENTLY	Define yourself by the problems you solve versus the products you make.
COMMUNICATE DIFFERENTLY	Align all aspects of marketing execution with a well-defined problem/solution framework.
ENGAGE DIFFERENTLY	Apply Solution Selling disciplines across all sales channels (direct and indirect).
REINFORCE DIFFERENTLY	Provide comprehensive support for solution-centric disciplines.

Once you've developed a compelling value framework and messaging platform and validated the markets and channels for problems you solve, you can focus on communicating the story differently both internally and externally.

Do Internal Communications Drive the Right Solution Priorities? Inevitably, there are more ideas on what products to make or improve upon in most companies than there are resources to apply to the task. One of the most daunting challenges in product marketing and management is setting appropriate priorities for scarce resources. While we will not delve deeply into product development in this book, it is important to have *internal* marketing "templates" and processes to keep the organization centered on problem solving and value defensibility. A rigorous understanding of customer problems and value defensibility should internally drive solution definitions and priorities.

In competitive environments, this is often extremely difficult because there is constant pressure to maintain parity with perceived rivals in the marketplace. To ensure that value defensibility drives product and service priorities, internal marketing communications, such as marketing requirements documents, need to consider customer value impact extensively. In Part Four, we provide some parameters and templates that help to ensure appropriate emphasis on customer problem relevance and value defensibility.

Are External Communications in Alignment with Sales Conversations? When we ask salespeople to have problem-focused dialogues with customers, it's important that we consider the extent to which all other forms of marketing communications consistently support the conversations that need to occur during the sell. Some examples of these forms of communication can be found in Figure 5.2. Customers form their perception of who we are through multiple communications channels, all of which need to be in sync.

Our story shouldn't be about how great and wonderful our company and our products are. Instead, it needs to

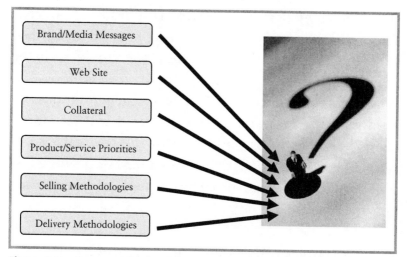

Figure 5.2 Forms of External Communication to the Customer

connect the relevance of our existence to the problems and needs of the customer. If you retain agencies, the tendency to be clever and memorable can take precedence over customer relevance. In many cases, sales operations or the sales force itself is left to translate marketing materials into value-based discussions with customers. In order to support Solution Selling methods effectively in the field, it's crucial to align multiple forms of marketing communications, including the Web site, collateral, public relations, and advertising, in parallel with the sales approach. In Part Four, we discuss major areas of marketing communications and alignment criteria.

Do We Launch Problems or Products?   Lead generation is surfacing as one of the top challenges in today's demand-poor environment. So when we launch something, we want the campaign to create as many leads as possible. Given that customers are primarily concerned about their problems, not about our offerings, we should focus on "launching problems for which we have a solution," as opposed to traditional products, pseudo-solutions, or even real solutions. Yet all too often, we still see launch campaigns that focus on how great the new offering is, not on how well the offering solves a buyer's problems. In Part Four, we discuss problem-focused lead generation concepts.

Companies must shed their product/feature orientations at critical aspects of the introduction process.

Are Key Messages and Differentiators Translated into Useful Sales Tools? All the hard work in developing a compelling value framework and messaging platform remains largely unleveraged unless it translates into practical tools and templates for salespeople—tools that really help them to reach the right types of buyers and engage successfully. The failure to build this bridge effectively is one of the biggest contributors to the marketing and sales disconnect that is so prevalent. Making this handoff successfully is pivotal in combating the low usage of marketing materials by sales organizations. In Part Four, we provide methods and templates that help to drive key elements of the messaging platform and value framework into specific sales tools.

Summary   Changing how we communicate aligns our conversations to the marketplace around the *conceptual* framework that is problem-solution oriented. This ensures the right type of "air cover" and message reinforcement for effective selling activities.

Transformation 3: Changing How You Engage

THINK DIFFERENTLY	Define yourself by the problems you solve versus the products you make.
COMMUNICATE DIFFERENTLY	Align all aspects of marketing execution with a well-defined problem/solution framework.
ENGAGE DIFFERENTLY	Apply Solution Selling disciplines across all sales channels (direct and indirect).
REINFORCE DIFFERENTLY	Provide comprehensive support for solution-centric disciplines.

While Solution Selling may be primarily thought of as sales training for individual salespeople, there is much more to adopting this approach to selling than simply providing training. The sales organization as a whole needs to understand and implement greater levels of process and methodology in order to optimize the use of resources and carry the problem-solving conversation effectively to the right buying sponsors. Key aspects of effective engagement are described in the following.

Do We Consistently Pursue the Right Types of Opportunities? When moving to a solutions approach, as we previously mentioned, there is a need to validate whether the appropriate market targets are being pursued. In other words, do the problems we solve have high relevance to the market segments that we intend to pursue?

Typically, market segmentation will feed into an overall territory plan that ultimately consists of a specific population of assigned accounts for salespeople. At both a sales team and individual level, it is important to apply a structured approach to determine the highest-probability accounts to pursue. This requires thoughtful consideration of the problems that are being addressed and determination of the specific characteristics of target companies that suggest high receptivity to key value messages. In Part Four, we discuss effective territory planning criteria and prioritization methods.

Do We Leverage Existing Customer Relationships Effectively? One of the major benefits of the solutions approach is that additional value-added offerings can be extended to existing customers to increase wallet share and lifetime customer value. Accomplishing revenue expansion into existing accounts, however, often requires a more rigorous approach and a more comprehensive understanding of the buying organization. In Part Four, we discuss effective account planning and management criteria and coverage concepts. The coverage concepts have to do with how well your team members are aligned with members of a client account.

Do We Understand How to Navigate Large, Complex Opportunities? The transition to selling solutions also tends to result in sales opportunities that are both larger and more complex. There are typically more selling and buying participants involved in the opportunity and greater complexity in the solution offering. The ability to consistently marshal the appropriate resources and navigate the buying process requires expanded rigor and organizational skills. In Part Four, we discuss criteria and tools for effective opportunity planning and management.

Do Individuals Have the Right Types of Skills and Knowledge? While throughout the course of this book we have emphasized that sales performance problems are not solely the result of individual skills deficiencies, these skills are still very much a factor in successful selling. The transition to solution selling requires a somewhat different profile and skill set than successful product salespeople may have. In Part Four, we discuss specific skills and knowledge required at the individual level to effectively sell solutions.

Summary   Changing how we engage customers calibrates how we prioritize potential opportunities with our actual problem-solving capabilities. In addition, this change also requires much greater rigor and discipline with respect to leveraging major account potential, as well as maximizing our win potential in large opportunities. Finally, new types of skills and knowledge are necessary to be perceived as a credible partner by the customer.

Transformation 4: Changing How You Reinforce

THINK DIFFERENTLY	Define yourself by the problems you solve versus the products you make.
COMMUNICATE DIFFERENTLY	Align all aspects of marketing execution with a well-defined problem/solution framework.
ENGAGE DIFFERENTLY	Apply Solution Selling disciplines across all sales channels (direct and indirect).
REINFORCE DIFFERENTLY	Provide comprehensive support for solution-centric disciplines.

Reinforcement is often the most neglected aspect of making a behavioral transformation. As we mentioned earlier, without the appropriate reinforcement vehicles, research indicates that within three months, 86 percent of skills and knowledge acquired through sales training is lost. Making the transition to a solution-centric organization requires formal reinforcement in multiple dimensions of the organization, as described in the following.

Does Sales Management Provide the Right Mentoring and Leadership? An essential part of reinforcement is about having managers and executives consistently encourage and enforce solution-centric concepts, principles, sales tools, and processes. Sales managers at every level need to understand the essence of solution-centric behavior and exactly how, where, when, and why they can support their salespeople in having more productive solution-oriented conversations with buyers. And they need to be encouraged by senior sales executives to do the right coaching, consistently and frequently.

Mentoring and effective leadership are two essentials in a solution-centric organization.

Because *what gets measured gets done*, a company's sales pipeline and performance measurement systems must reinforce all the basic elements of the solution-centric approach—and leave no room for misinterpretation or mixed messages about what management expects salespeople to do, when they should do it, why they need to do it, and how they need to do it. In Part Four, we discuss criteria for effective sales management and leadership.

Are Our Recruiting Practices and Organizational Design Aligned with a Solution-Centric Mindset? Recruits into a solution-centric organization need to be able, prepared, and motivated to conduct different conversations than simply describing product features and benefits. They need to be intrinsically motivated by the challenges of diagnosing buyers' problems, navigating their way through the organization to find and work with the influencers and decision makers, and determining which solution(s) will address the customer's business problems most cost-effectively. Navigating this type of process requires a very different type of aptitude than traditional product selling skills, so recruiting efforts need to be reconfigured to find, attract, and hire such people.

Fortunately, there are now online assessments that can help to test for specific aptitudes, which can help identify people who are better equipped to sell solutions. Similarly, marketing, sales, business development, and customer services organizations may all need to be reconfigured to support a solution-centric approach—at the extreme, possibly grouping all those functions together by solution type, as opposed to by function, product, or technology type or customer type. In Part Four, we discuss organizational design issues and criteria.

How Do We Compensate and Reward People? Aligning compensation and reward programs with a solution-centric approach involves ensuring that behaviors that lead to more solution sales are rewarded. For example, this may require a shift from individual bonuses to team bonuses, since often complex solutions cannot be sold by the lone-wolf sales star. The range of bonuses may expand to incorporate new players, such as industry experts who are brought in to advise on aspects of a solution as part of the sales process. It may require less incentive compensation and more fixed salary so that salespeople feel comfortable devoting time to the longer sales cycles that solution sales often demand. It may even require defining new ways of rewarding salespeople—for example, making compensation based on value created for the *customer* by selling a solution as opposed to value created for the selling company. Ultimately, long-term value created for and recognized by the customer should be more important in a truly solution-centric organization than short-term value created for the salespeople. In Part Four, we review criteria for compensation and performance management.

Do We Apply Technology to Effectively Support Our Problem-Solving Capabilities? We have already mentioned several applications of technology in reinforcing solution-centric behavior, such as restructuring Web sites around solutions, not products and features, and incorporating solution-centric behavior into sales pipeline monitoring and sales forecasting systems. In addition, solution-centric behavior can be reinforced through creative use of CRM and sales support systems that enhance the problem-solving capabilities of the overall selling team—for example, use of knowledge management systems that document and provide ready user-friendly access to databases of company experience that are searchable by problem type or symptom. Many top professional services firms, such as consulting and accounting firms, have such searchable databases because they recognize that storing knowledge about past solutions to client problems is often vital to the next sales initiative. A variety of other industries also now use knowledge management systems to codify and access previous experience so that everyone in the organization can leverage knowledge about past problems solved. In Part Four, we discuss concepts and criteria for effective technology application.

Does Our Culture and Leadership Reinforce Our Commitment to Solution-Centric Behavior Style? It's not just the sales organization or even the marketing organization that needs to get behind the solution-centric thrust. All companies can provide a tally of products sold in a given year, but how many can accurately report on how many customer problems they actually solved or what the customer impact of each solution was? Highlighting and lauding problems solved for leading customers is one of the ways in which companies can begin to change an old product-focused culture toward a more solution-centric one. Making a team that has solved a large flagship customer's core problem the centerpiece of an employee newsletter—or even better, sometimes an annual report—is a tactic that many a company has adopted. Similarly, a series of CEO-level recognition events about solution-centric successes can have a substantial impact on employees and the organization's long-term culture. In Part Four, we review leadership and cultural criteria to support a solution-centric transformation.

Summary While the term *reinforcement* may sound rather mundane, building appropriate reinforcement vehicles is the essential "adhesive" that drives sustainable change. Effective reinforcement covers multiple dimensions of the business, including mentoring and coaching, organizational design, technology application, and culture and leadership styles.

A PRACTICAL FRAMEWORK TO DRIVE PERFORMANCE IMPROVEMENT

THE VALUE PERCEPTION GAP

Since informed customers aren't willing to pay for value they don't perceive, the company's perceived value can't be monetized as revenues, let alone as profits.

*The attempt to resolve a perceived problem
is a reaction that is largely focused
on the symptom, not on the underlying
cause(s) of the symptom.*

VALUE INVISIBILITY

In Chapter Five, we reviewed solution-transformation from a conceptual perspective: How do we need to change the way that we think, communicate, engage, and reinforce? While this conceptual overview is a useful step to organize our thinking and begin to determine the extent to which we are solution-centric, the question remains: How do we put these concepts and principles into practice coherently? In other words, how do we translate these concepts into a *systemic* approach that provides a broader methodology for effectively marketing and selling solutions? It's useful to step back and revisit the fundamental problem at hand. Most companies have an underlying goal of sustainable revenue growth and, linked to that, sustainable sales performance improvement. One way to frame the high-level problem from a systemic perspective is a concept that we briefly discussed in Part One and that many companies can relate to—*value invisibility*.

Companies think that their offerings to the marketplace deliver value, but somehow that perception doesn't connect with their prospects and customers. In essence, the inherent value of the offering isn't *visible* or tangible enough to stimulate action on the part of the buyer. Because increasingly informed customers aren't willing to pay for value that *they* don't perceive, the company's perceived value can't be captured fully and monetized as revenues, let alone as profits.

If customers do not clearly recognize tangible, or measurable, differences in your offerings, they will not see a unique value proposition or a reason to buy.

In simplest terms, the inability to grow sales revenues means that not enough buyers are choosing offerings at a profitable price point. Either they aren't buying at all, or they are opting for an alternative, or they are unwilling to agree to a price point that is necessary to sustain acceptable profitability.

A number of industry findings tend to bear out the value perception challenge as illustrated in Figure 6.1. Somewhere between the core value proposition and the point of sale, something is broken. The questions are, "Where are the breakdowns occurring, and what is causing them?"

In many cases, the attempt to resolve a perceived problem is a reaction that is largely focused on the symptom, not on the underlying cause(s) of the symptom. What do we mean by this? As an example, suppose an organization is experiencing difficulty engaging with senior-level executives and accessing buying power consistently. A common

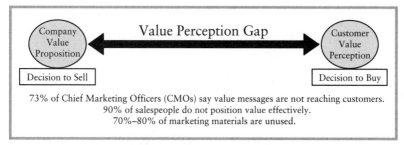

Figure 6.1 Value Perception Gap

assumption might be that salespeople lack the requisite skills to engage effectively with executive buying sponsors. The reaction to this assumption would typically be investment in sales training on techniques that focus on how to sell more effectively to executives. It's not necessarily a bad idea—this type of training may in fact be essential or even critical in addressing the problem. But a deeper analysis of the problem might uncover a number of other *significant* factors at play as well, including one or more of the following:

- The actual value proposition for the offering may not be defensible or compelling at the senior executive level.
- Key messages may not have relevance to the appropriate power sponsors.
- Segmentation and targeting may be suboptimal for the business problems being addressed, resulting in poor message receptivity.
- Sales channels may not be appropriate for the actual customer problems and needs being addressed.
- Marketing communications may be product superiority–focused versus business issue–focused.

- Lead generation may focus on product features and functions versus critical business issues that resonate with executive sponsors.
- Sales managers may lack the coaching and mentoring skills necessary to provide meaningful assistance in the sales process.
- Organizational design may not be aligned to sell effectively into the "problem domain" of the potential buyers (i.e., specialized sales resources may be required but are not available).
- Territory and account management disciplines may not be in place to ensure effective focus on qualified buyers.

In other words, before "adjusting the dials," it is critical to have accurate insight into the causal factors of the problem being experienced. Again, as the findings of Primary Intelligence indicate, in many cases, organizations tend to guess wrong about the actual causes of sales performance problems.

THE SIX SYSTEMIC DRIVERS
(BARRIERS) OF VALUE PERCEPTION

So how do we minimize the probabilities of guessing wrong? Or, put another way, how do we better apply principles of management science to improving sales performance? As we have noted on several occasions, a common reaction to the types of problems just outlined is to assume that there is a single localized issue within the sales force.

While this may be the case, in our experience we have observed six, not just one, principal causes for these very common revenue growth problems. How well a company deals with these causes either enables or inhibits its ability to drive and sustain sales revenue increases. Figure 6.2 illustrates the six systemic drivers of sales performance improvement, three of which are related to marketing alignment (above the funnel), and three of which pertain to sales execution (in the funnel).

1. *Value framework and messaging.* This is the extent to which value positioning and messages are defined around accurately perceived customer problems and needs, not around products and services. Does the way the company defines its offerings resonate with customers as addressing their problems versus pushing products? This is the "aiming of the gun," so to speak—if the purpose of the company isn't *explicitly* about solving problems and meeting needs at the highest level, then value dilution occurs at every point thereafter.

2. *Targeted go-to-market approach.* This is the degree to which a company's value propositions, market seg-

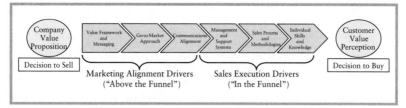

Figure 6.2 Systemic Drivers of Value Perception

mentation approach, and channel strategies should be attuned with customers' perceived needs. Is the go-to-market approach in sync with real customer problems and needs, and are selling channels appropriate? In other words, market segments and channels need to be calibrated with a problem-solving orientation.

3. *Aligned marketing communications.* This is the degree to which marketing communications and lead generation are aligned properly with field sales conversations. Are marketing communications consistently in parallel with sales conversations? All forms of internal communications also need to convey and instill the concepts and principles of a problem-solving organization.

4. *Management support systems.* This it the caliber and consistent use of management vehicles to improve skills and reinforce sales processes. Do management practices, technology, compensation, and culture reinforce the desired selling approach? Sales managers can't just crunch the pipeline numbers—effective teams require real coaching and mentoring. Technology needs to enable improved problem diagnosis and vision creation, and compensation needs to consider customer outcomes in addition to internal metrics.

5. *A codified sales process and methodologies.* This is the presence of a formal sales process that aligns well with customers' typical buying processes. Are selling processes well defined, understood, practiced, and supported in ways that align with the way that buyers buy? Here we refer again to the recent IDC observation: "The days of the lone-wolf sales star are numbered." The more com-

plex the problem and the corresponding solution, the greater the need for effective team collaboration. Winging it won't cut it in complex, highly competitive selling environments—teams need to understand the playbook and be able to execute accordingly.

6. *Skills and knowledge to engage with customers.* This is the quality of fundamental selling skills and knowledge at the individual salesperson level. Can salespeople effectively diagnose customer problems and needs and create a vision of the solution that the customer will buy? Even if your solutions have compelling value and attract great levels of interest, it's still quite possible to lose at the end of the sale. Individual salespeople need to be highly literate with respect to both customer problems and the linkages to the appropriate capabilities.

In essence, to really get the revenue engine into high gear, one needs to thoughtfully align key aspects of above-the-funnel marketing drivers with in-the-funnel sales execution drivers.

When the six systemic drivers are aligned tightly with customers' needs and each other, a company is positioned to sustain consistent sales revenue increases. When the drivers are misaligned, revenue generation problems are inevitable. With misalignment, a company's internal perception of the value it offers cannot reach its customers' perceptions of value—and the stage is set that fosters significant problems in differentiating and positioning your offerings, and commodity perceptions, and a host of symptoms and results of inefficient sales efforts. It's important to note that we're not talking about boiling the ocean here—we prefer to think in terms of a *recalibration* in key areas of sales and marketing to ensure the best probabilities of consistently winning.

THE SYSTEMIC COST OF MISCALCULATION

Before we delve more deeply into the six key performance drivers, let's consider how dramatically systemic misalignment can contribute to a host of potential performance problems, as well as cloud the real causes of those problems. An interesting analogy at this point comes to us from the software industry. Studies have shown that when software products fail to meet end-user requirements correctly, there are exponential cost ramifications when the problem is discovered subsequent to the actual design phase, as illustrated in Figure 6.3.

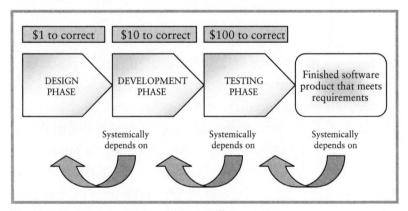

Figure 6.3   Consequences of Miscalculation

If incorrect design assumptions are made at the outset, there is a ripple effect that cascades into each subsequent phase of the process. Correcting the problem is significantly more complex and costly as the incorrect assumption makes its way deeper into the finished product. Why is this the case? In large part because a single design assumption can make its way into the code in dozens of places with high levels of interdependency.

Fixing "problems" becomes increasingly difficult—and increasingly expensive— as they work their way through the systems of the company.

The design concept becomes "codified" into the product, and unraveling the impact of the mistake can be daunting as well as disruptive to the remaining functionality. Ironically, many software defects are introduced by fixing other problems in the code. Localized tampering without understanding key interdependencies in the design can produce potentially disastrous consequences.

Now, let's think in terms of a process that takes us effectively from a value proposition to the point of sale. If a product-centric mindset is entrenched at the beginning of the process, there is a high probability that product-centric practices and behaviors will become highly codified in the makeup of the organization. If we simply attempt to address sales performance problems at the salesperson level, it is improbable that we will see the levels of sustainable improvement that we are seeking. In some cases, turning the wrong dials without understanding the underlying causes first can actually make salespeople less effective.

MAPPING PERFORMANCE PROBLEMS TO DRIVERS

Let's take the systemic thought process a step further. Earlier, we mentioned how companies can erroneously focus on symptoms of issues and not on the underlying cause itself. The chart in Figure 6.4 illustrates the systemic implications of 10 very common symptoms that companies tend to experience when sales aren't meeting expectations with respect to the six performance drivers.

Our analysis of these problems indicates that every one of them is impacted by some aspect of each of the six drivers, although there are varying degrees of influence across the drivers for each type of problem. The typical reaction to any of these problems might be to take some form of localized action.

For example, the "lack of qualified leads" might be typically perceived as a marketing campaign issue. While this area certainly merits some scrutiny, there are a number of other factors that could be contributing materially to the difficulty in building an adequate pipeline. Figure 6.5 illustrates a deeper look at where other systemic factors could be at play with respect to lead generation.

As we see in the example, each of the six systemic drivers can have an impact on the ability to consistently generate demand for your offerings. In addition, these systemic

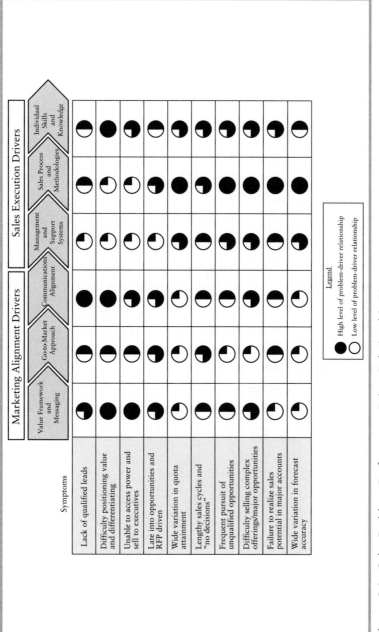

Figure 6.4   Sales Problem–Performance Driver Relationship Map

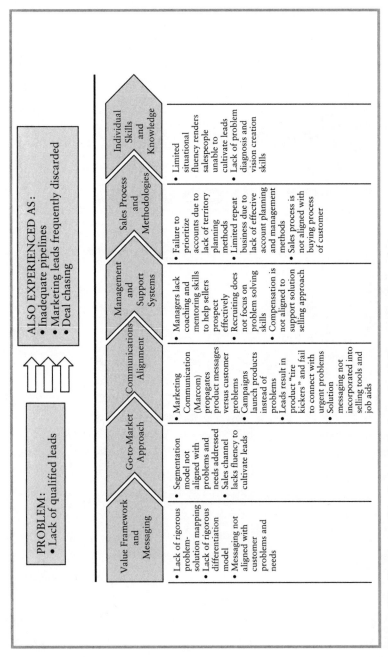

PROBLEM:
• Lack of qualified leads

ALSO EXPERIENCED AS:
• Inadequate pipelines
• Marketing leads frequently discarded
• Deal chasing

Value Framework and Messaging	Go-to-Market Approach	Communications Alignment	Management and Support Systems	Sales Process and Methodologies	Individual Skills and Knowledge
• Lack of rigorous problem-solution mapping • Lack of rigorous differentiation model • Messaging not aligned with customer problems and needs	• Segmentation model not aligned with problems and needs addressed • Sales channel lacks fluency to cultivate leads	• Marketing Communication (Marcom) propagates product messages versus customer problems • Campaigns launch products instead of problems • Leads result in product "tire kickers" and fail to connect with urgent problems • Solution messaging not incorporated into selling tools and job aids	• Managers lack coaching and mentoring skills to help sellers prospect effectively • Recruiting does not focus on problem solving skills • Compensation is not aligned to support solution selling approach	• Failure to prioritize accounts due to lack of territory planning methods • Limited repeat business due to lack of effective account planning and management methods • Sales process is not aligned with buying process of customer	• Limited situational fluency renders salespeople unable to cultivate leads • Lack of problem diagnosis and vision creation skills

Figure 6.5 Understanding Systemic Factors—Lead Generation Example

■ 116 ■

interdependencies can have a cascading impact. For example, the lack of rigor in understanding customer problems and needs can yield ineffective messages, incorrect assumptions about target markets, and product-focused campaigns that fail to connect in a compelling way with potential buyers. This may also impair situational fluency for salespeople and inhibit their ability to cultivate the leads that actually are generated. In other words, the lead generation function relies on multiple aspects of upstream and downstream effectiveness. In Chapter Seven, we explore the six systemic drivers and subfactors in greater detail.

THE SALES PERFORMANCE IMPROVEMENT FRAMEWORK

The assessment model that follows allows us to understand where specific barriers to performance exist, to evaluate their effect on a company's ability to grow the top line consistently, and to prescribe specific recommendations for improvement.

It is critical to understand the end-to-end health of the overall marketing and sales ecosystem in order to make intelligent adjustments.

THE SALES PERFORMANCE IMPROVEMENT FRAMEWORK: DRIVERS AND SUBFACTORS

The six systemic drivers discussed in Chapter Six comprise the basis for a rigorous diagnostic framework. They enable an objective assessment of the barriers to sustainable revenue and value growth from initial value concepts through point of sale. The methodology applies a structured approach to look systemically at everything from formulation of the value proposition through market and channel strategies, marketing communications, and the full spectrum of sales activities and processes. This assessment model allows us to understand where specific barriers to performance exist, to evaluate their effect on a company's ability to sustain revenue increases, and to prescribe specific recommendations for improvement.

Figure 7.1 shows the assessment model's three above-the-funnel market alignment drivers, the three in-the-funnel sales execution drivers, and the 24 respective subfactors. The figure also positions the four fundamental transformations that need to occur as discussed in Chapter Six.

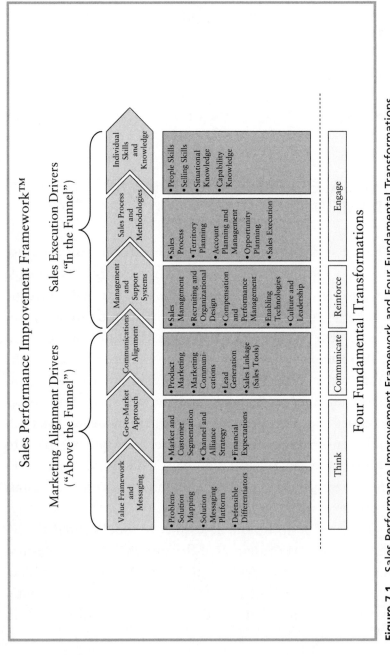

Figure 7.1 Sales Performance Improvement Framework and Four Fundamental Transformations

Notice how the four conceptual transformations, discussed in Part Two, relate closely to the six systemic drivers; in addition, as we move from right to left, we are involving more areas of the overall sales and marketing organizations; and as we move from left to right in the framework, we are moving progressively from the strategic to the tactical. The systemic cost of miscalculation is exponentially higher the further to the left it occurs.

If we make erroneous assumptions about the problems we actually solve, we are much more likely to make segmentation and sales channel mistakes and much less likely to formulate the right solutions, and marketing communications and lead generation will lack customer relevance. In turn, these problems will cascade into all aspects of downstream sales execution. In short, it is critical to understand the end-to-end health of the overall marketing and sales ecosystem in order to make intelligent adjustments. In the following paragraphs, we will explore each of the performance drivers and their subcomponents in greater detail.

First, we will discuss the framework's drivers and subfactors at a high level, and in Part Four, we will apply a diagnostic methodology as we delve deeper into those drivers and subfactors.

The Marketing and Sales Ecosystem

1. The Value Framework and Messaging Platform
2. The Go-to-Market Approach
3. Communications Alignment

4. Management and Support Systems
5. Sales Process and Methodologies
6. Individual Skills and Knowledge

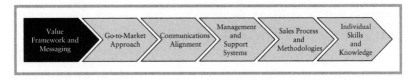

The *value framework* and *messaging platform* has three fundamental components:

- *Problem-solution mapping.* The first step in understanding your value proposition is to develop a comprehensive, rigorous inventory of customer problems, needs, and opportunities. The idea here is to assess the match between customer problems or needs that an organization can legitimately address and the positioning of the company's solutions.
- *Defensible differentiators.* In many cases, companies fail to build a formal and structured model of differentiated positioning and confuse features, functions, and characteristics of their product or service with real differentiators. Companies need a *structured* way to assess their offerings versus their competitors' so that they can see clearly where and how they can leverage differences that are of real value to customers.
- *The solution messaging platform.* The overall messaging platform focuses on the most critical needs and problems facing its customers—which allows cus-

tomers to relate easily to the stated problems and see clearly how the solution addresses those problems.

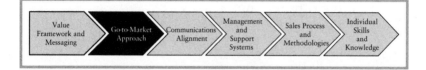

The *go-to-market approach* also has three fundamental components:

- *Market and customer segmentation approach.* A company needs to determine whether it has defined its go-to-market approach around existing products and services, as opposed to around the customer problems it solves. In such cases, it is critical to revisit the problem-solution mapping and to carefully identify those market segments that are best served by the problems the company actually solves.
- *Channel and alliance strategy.* It is essential to identify the direct and indirect sales channels that can *competently* take solutions capabilities into the marketplace. Internal and external sales channels need to be capable of diagnosing customer problems effectively and creating a coherent vision of the solution by aligning capabilities insightfully.
- *Financial expectations.* As a shift to selling solutions takes place, it is important to consider thoughtfully how specific offerings that address significant customer needs will make their way into the marketplace and generate revenue across the old lines of

reporting by product and/or geography. It is critical to rationalize the strategic revenue forecast in a solutions context, considering segmentation, channels, and the offering mix.

Communications alignment involves aligning all aspects of internal and external communications with the problems and needs defined in the value framework and messaging platform. It has four components:

- *Product marketing.* Product marketing communications need to be grounded in real problems that customers value solving—and product marketing and management priorities need to factor customer value heavily into their decision processes. Traditional methods of identifying market potential for offerings are still essential, but it is equally critical to understand how much customer value results from providing a particular set of capabilities—well before investing in product and service development.
- *Marketing communications.* All aspects of corporate communications to the external world must align with the problems that the organization solves, not align with the products that it makes or sells. Web sites, Marcom collateral, advertising, white papers, analyst interactions, and other media relations activities—in

fact, any decision on how and what will be communicated to the external world in any medium or channel—should be consistent with real customer problems that are solved and actual needs that are addressed.

- *Lead generation.* In many cases, marketing campaigns and lead generation efforts are based on the release of a product or service, as opposed to being focused on new abilities to solve significant customer problems. In order to create urgency and expose latent pain, lead generation programs should focus on the problems that salespeople should be exploring with customers as they attempt to uncover the value potential of real customer need.

- *Sales linkage and sales tools.* All the best messaging, marketing, and product management ideas make their way into practical and usable sales tools that the field sales organization and channel organizations can use. If making this translation is not taken seriously, all the other hard solution-centric work upstream goes to waste.

Next are the three in-the-funnel sales execution drivers.

Management and support systems. Sales management and support systems need to ensure that all sales resources are given adequate direction and support to achieve the company's sales and other strategic goals. Companies typically need to assess the following dimensions of their sales management and support systems:

- *Sales management.* Sales management should know how to lead, motivate, and coach salespeople so as to continuously improve sales performance and the achievement of other strategic goals. Management practices should consistently reinforce all the key aspects of desired solution-centric sales force behaviors.
- *Recruiting and organizational design.* Recruiting practices need to be aligned with the appropriate professional profiles to effectively represent the company's solutions. Organizational design may need to be recalibrated to support the expertise required to engage with new types of buyers.
- *Compensation and performance management.* Compensation and reward structures should reinforce and reward the most important solution-centric behaviors through well-communicated and accurately measured programs.
- *Enabling technologies.* Technology tools need to be applied in ways that enhance organizational problem-solving capabilities, not simply as a tool for management oversight or forecasting.
- *Culture and leadership.* Organizational culture and leadership are the essential ingredients in making the transition to a solution-centric organization. Key leadership roles need to reflect the commitment to being a problem-solving organization by executing

the agenda for change and enforcing the principles required to continue the transformation.

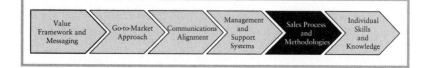

Sales process and methodologies. A company's formal sales methodology should ensure that the sales process and the buying process are well aligned and calibrated to one another in every dimension of being solution-centric.

- *Territory planning.* Territory planning should occur in a rigorous and structured way to make certain that salespeople face the right amount of market potential in each territory, that they identify the highest-potential targets in their territories, and that they pursue those potential opportunities in an efficient way to achieve optimal sales results.
- *Account planning and management.* Once a viable prospective customer has been identified, a company's account planning and management process should enable it to capture as much of the opportunity at that customer as possible. A formal account planning and management process can help salespeople and sales teams to identify and act on the best potential solution opportunities in established accounts.
- *Opportunity planning.* It's very important to under-stand how to navigate effectively through the organizational intricacies involved in selling complex solu-

tions. A sound opportunity planning and management methodology helps to guide salespeople or sales teams through intricate buyer decision processes, qualifying opportunities before investing significant resources and ensuring a structured and effective approach to the pursuit of those opportunities.

- *Sales execution.* Sales processes do not stand alone—they are surrounded by other interlocking processes that support and influence the sales function's success. Typically, sales processes need to be integrated closely with CRM and customer service functions—and each of these processes needs to be aligned with customer buying processes for complex solutions.

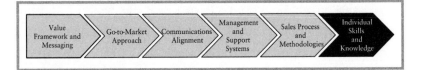

Individual skills and knowledge. Sales professionals and individuals in the channel need to have the appropriate skills and knowledge in four areas to function well:

- *People skills.* Effective salespeople of complex solutions typically demonstrate a genuine approach to building rapport with customers and understanding and relating to a customer's individual situation and specific pains.
- *Selling skills.* Effective salespeople have the fundamental ability and discipline to use a sales methodology consistently to diagnose customer problems accurately,

create visions of solutions, and lead the customer through the buying process.

- *Situational knowledge.* Effective salespeople are able to demonstrate a broad knowledge of the business issues and industry trends a customer faces based on the customer's marketplace and environment. They are adept at connecting a customer's situation and primary pains with how solutions will address the problems.
- *Capabilities knowledge.* Effective salespeople need exceptional knowledge of their offerings and capabilities in order to identify which solution components are most important to any specific customer.

ORGANIZATIONAL IMPLICATIONS

In previous sections, we have illustrated solution-centricity from two dimensions: (1) a conceptual view, where four key areas of overall transformation were discussed at a high level: changing how you think, changing how you communicate, changing how you engage, and changing how you reinforce; and (2) a systemic view, where we discussed a framework that defines a set of systemic drivers from the value proposition through the point-of-sales interaction.

The old cliché "everyone is a salesperson" holds meaningful ramifications for the solution-centric organization.

We would be remiss to omit a discussion of the organizational aspects of making this transformation. While the majority of this book focuses on the *revenue engine*, which primarily involves the sales and marketing organizations, some of our clients have realized, appropriately, that making the transformation to solution-centric has implications that go beyond those two organizations. The old saying "everyone is a salesperson" is a cliché, but many areas of the company *can* materially contribute to the marketing and sales of high-value solutions. To that end, the illustration in Figure 7.2 provides a high-level mapping of organizational involvement in the Sales Performance Improvement Framework.

It is important to make several observations at this point. First, readers may note that there is no organizational representation for engineering, manufacturing, and services and delivery functions. While there are clearly many synergies and alignment concepts that apply to these functional areas, we have attempted to apply the 80/20 rule and focus on a set of transformational ideas and systemic drivers that have broad applicability across industries and markets. In other words, whether you are a manufacturing company, a services firm, or a bank, the marketing alignment and sales execution drivers we have defined have relevance.

In future papers and books, we will likely explore additional functional areas that have more industry-specific characteristics. That is, how a bank formulates products and services into solutions may vary significantly from how a manufacturer does the same thing. However, both

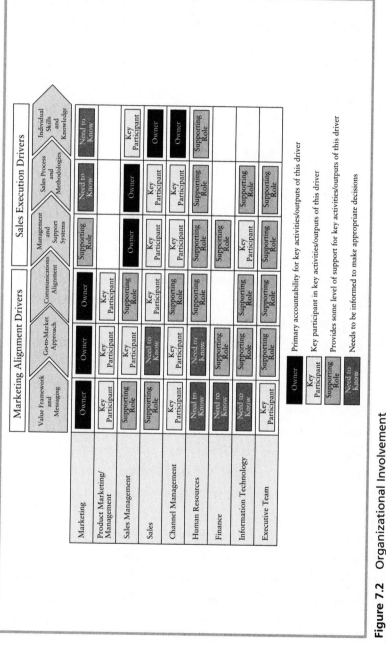

Figure 7.2 Organizational Involvement

types of organizations need to develop a comprehensive understanding of the customer problems that they solve, determine the best target segments and channels, etc. Adoption of a systemic framework in the areas we have defined will likely provide clues and insights into changes that need to take place in functional areas beyond those illustrated in Figure 7.2.

Secondly, the diagram is illustrative—it is not intended to depict a recommended organizational structure chart. Rather, we have highlighted some key functional areas that commonly exist in many companies and how those areas play a role across the six marketing alignment and sales execution drivers. For example, in some companies, product marketing and management fall under marketing, while in others, they may not. Here we have broken out *product marketing/management* from *marketing*—in this view of the organization, we see marketing as the *conceptual* definer of the problem-solution understanding, while the role of product marketing/management is to translate those ideas into usable solutions in an optimal manner for the organization.

Also, we have broken out *sales management* and *sales*—primarily because we think that sales management has some distinct accountabilities in a solution-centric environment that merit their own placeholder. Again, readers can extrapolate to apply concepts appropriately to their own organizations. In all probability, these concepts will lead to some level of organizational recalibration, both in organizational design and skills and knowledge profiles. In Chapter Fourteen, we provide a set of checklists for organizational accountabilities for each of the six performance drivers in the framework.

THE SALES PERFORMANCE HEALTH CHECK

Now that we've reviewed the overall performance framework, we can apply it to perform an overall sales performance health check. Figure 7.3 illustrates a sample "dashboard" that provides a high-level view of the overall state of an example revenue engine. This output is the result of an assessment of key subfactors within each of the six performance drivers and indicates the health status of each of the drivers, as well as that of each subfactor. At a glance, we can quickly zero in on areas of sales performance that are the most probable causes for problems being experienced.

In the chapters that follow, we will discuss relevant considerations for each of the performance drivers and review the assessment criteria that guide our health ratings. In addition to presenting fundamental diagnostic questions for each area, we also include illustrative examples that can be used to build templates in key areas that can help to establish improved rigor in the understanding of customer problems and needs.

Chapters Eight through Ten address the performance drivers and subfactors for marketing alignment, and Chapters Eleven through Thirteen address sales execution performance drivers and subfactors. Chapter Fourteen provides a model that helps define specific accountabilities across functional areas within an organization. To perform

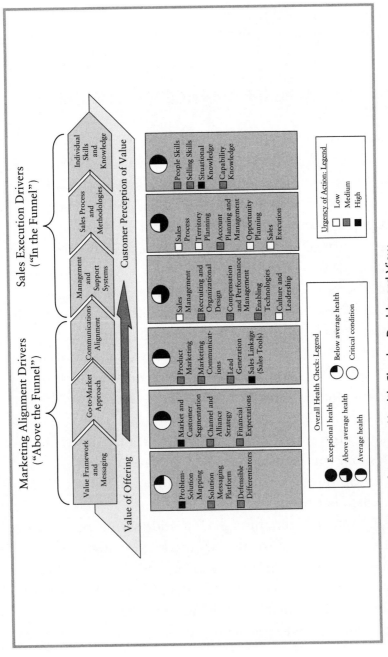

Figure 7.3 Sample Sales Performance Health Check—Dashboard View

an overall health check for your organization, have appropriate members of the marketing and sales teams use the health check questions to review each performance driver and its subfactors. By assessing the extent to which the criteria in each area are currently met, it should be possible to identify specific areas where performance gaps exist.

It is important to recognize that at this point in time, no framework is perfect and no concepts apply universally to all situations. In this book, we have tried to find a starting point for companies to begin a meaningful transition from being product-centric to solution-centric.

P A R T
F O U R

SALES PERFORMANCE HEALTH CHECK

PREFACE—PART FOUR

The first three parts of this book provided a more traditional reading experience and dealt with an executive-level view of *what* it means to be solution-centric. Part Four of this book is different; as a reader, you will see a departure in both style and content. Part Four deals with *how* to apply the solution-centric concepts by providing a detailed set of assessment criteria checklists or models that can be used by your organization to evaluate where potential sales performance gaps exist. In addition, it provides numerous templates and tools that can be applied to adopt a more solution-centric approach. In short, Part Four becomes a workbook for the concepts.

Chapters Eight to Ten focus on marketing alignment drivers—the assessment checklists in these chapters can be used by your product marketing and marketing teams to assess specific areas of marketing alignment that contribute to effective overall sales performance. Chapters Eleven to Thirteen focus on sales execution drivers—the assessment checklists in these chapters can be used by sales management and operations to assess key aspects of sales effectiveness. Chapter Fourteen provides a model for organizational involvement and accountability recommendations across each of the six performance drivers. The recommendations can be used to define roles and responsibilities across key functional areas to support a solution-centric transformation.

Part Four fulfills our desire to distinguish this book from just another executive-read on business concepts and outlines *how* to apply them. The rest is up to you. We encourage you to roll up your sleeves and engage the appropriate functional groups within your organization to utilize these checklists, templates, and tools.

THE VALUE FRAMEWORK AND MESSAGING PLATFORM

*The development of a rigorous
problem-solution map is a prerequisite
to putting together an effective
solution-oriented messaging platform.*

By getting the right answers to the right questions, you lay the groundwork for high levels of situational fluencies in all your customer conversations— whether they originate in marketing or the sales organization.

THIS AREA OF THE HEALTH CHECK is performed to ensure that a rigorous approach to understanding customer problems and needs is taken. In addition, it is important to assess the approach to defining defensible differentiators. These activities are the foundation for creating a compelling value proposition and solution messaging platform.

THE VALUE FRAMEWORK AND MESSAGING PLATFORM HEALTH CHECK

The foundation for creating a compelling value-proposition and solution messaging platform lies in thoroughly understanding customer problems and needs and applying a structured approach to defining defensible differentiators.

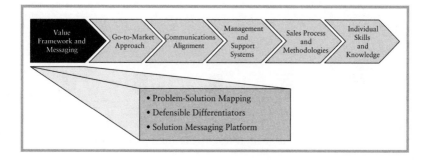

PROBLEM-SOLUTION MAPPING

Here, we are assessing the extent to which we truly understand the *problem state* facing the customer. That is, what *specific* problems, needs, and challenges is the customer potentially experiencing? We need to be able to do more than just identify problems—we need to also assess how well we link specific causes of each type of customer problem and its impact on customer operations and finances, and how our solution components actually address those customer problems. From a scope perspective, we suggest that problem-solution mapping be developed for each distinct market segment.

By investing in the answers to these questions, we are laying the groundwork for high levels of situational fluency in all our customer conversations—whether they originate in marketing or the sales organization. Figure 8.1 demonstrates a high-level template for organizing the problem-solution mapping for a given market segment.

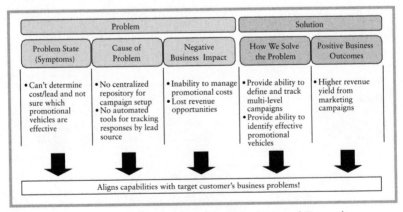

Figure 8.1   Problem-Solution Mapping Template and Example

ASSESSMENT CRITERIA FOR PROBLEM-SOLUTION MAPPING

- Is a *comprehensive* inventory of specific problems, needs, and opportunities defined for each key market segment?
- Are the causes (or drivers) for these problems identified clearly—do you understand what internal and external forces are leading to the specific problems?
- Is the business impact, from both an operational and financial perspective, clearly linked to specific problems in measurable terms?
- Are the consequences of delay or not addressing the problem clearly identified in measurable terms?
- Are specific capabilities that are required to address the actual *causes* of the problems clearly defined?
- Are the solution components that you provide clearly linked to specific capabilities required to solve problems?
- Are the positive business consequences and value of the solution clearly defined and defensible?
- Are the items enumerated above understood for specific buying sponsors?

DEFENSIBLE DIFFERENTIATORS

As we mentioned earlier, a brief, informal survey of cross-functional executives often reveals the lack of rigor in defining differentiators. In many cases features, functions, and characteristics of products or services are confused with real differentiators. After developing a comprehensive understanding of key problems that we address, it's important to assess the degree to which our points of differentiation are defensible and relevant to customers. In order to structure thinking around differentiation, we find it useful to consider differentiators in three specific categories: proprietary, comparative, and holistic.

1. *Proprietary differentiators* are items that are truly unique, that no competitor offers. In the long run, they are the most defensible form of differentiator.
2. *Comparative differentiators* are specific capabilities that competitors also offer, but where a company's offer is better than the alternatives in some or many aspects.
3. *Holistic differentiators* reflect overall ways in which it is much more attractive to do business with our company than with the competition (e.g., in overall financial terms and conditions and in number of regional locations).

For each distinct differentiator, it is essential to validate two other aspects of differentiation: the actual defensibility of differentiation claims, as well as the customer value of differentiators.

A helpful tool for defining the differentiation framework can be found in Figure 8.2. The Defensible Differentiation Template organizes differentiators into three categories and relates differentiators to specific critical business issues

(CBIs), customer value impact, and defensibility factors. The comparative section can be broken out by key competitors to highlight specific advantages for each.

ASSESSMENT CRITERIA FOR DEFENSIBLE DIFFERENTIATORS

- Are proprietary differentiators clearly enumerated? These are the attributes of solution offering(s) that are truly unique and no competitor offers.
- Are comparative differentiators identified and rigorously compared to specific competitive claims of similar capability?
- Are holistic differentiators insightfully identified (have all the key advantages of why it is attractive to do business with your company been thoughtfully identified)?
- Is the defensibility of each differentiation claim clearly defined and legitimate?
- Is the relationship to customer pain and value of each differentiator clearly understood?
- Is the differentiation platform published and understood by the entire organization?

THE SOLUTION MESSAGING PLATFORM

Since an effective solution-oriented messaging platform should focus on the most critical needs and problems fac-

Differentiator	CBI/Pain Linkage	Value Impact	Defensibility
Proprietary			
Campaign Analyzer	Inability to determine relative effectiveness of campaigns	• Improved targeting capabilities • Reduced cost/lead • Higher conversion rates	Patent pending (2005)
Differentiator 2			
Differentiator 3			
Comparative—Competitor 1			
Data import capabilities—we have superior, visual data-mapping toolset	• Time and cost to synchronize CRM and marketing data • Lower response rates due to inaccurate data	• Improved response rates • Reduced cost of ownership	• We provide free proof-of-concept to import customer data (our competitors won't do this)
Differentiator 2			
Differentiator 3			
Holistic			
Regional service offices in 14 major metropolitan areas	Difficulty getting timely, hands-on assistance and coaching	Improved use of tools and analysis capabilities	Received Information World's highest service rating for enterprise software companies
Differentiator 2			
Differentiator 3			

Figure 8.2   Defensible Differentiation Template

150

ing a company's customers, the development of a rigorous problem-solution mapping and differentiation framework is a fundamental prerequisite. In many cases, the problem/solution mapping may generate 40 to 50 specific problems. Since effective messaging needs to be concise, the challenge is to distill the problem inventory into a manageable set of high-level business issues. In most cases, logical groupings emerge from the problem-solution mapping. In addition to being problem-focused, it is also important for messages to have relevance to key top-of-mind issues for customers, and to leverage key differentiation points as well. It's vital to assess the overall messaging platform to ensure that our conversations, whether in sales or through marketing communications, are connecting with key problems and issues.

The challenge is to distill the problem inventory into a definable set of high-level business issues.

Two templates that help to develop problem-focused messages are the Critical Business Issue (CBI) Menu and Solution Messaging Cards. The CBI Menu provides a high-level set of key conversation points that ensure consistency in framing the problems we solve for customers. It essentially distills the overall problem inventory (developed in the problem-solution mapping) into a concise set of issues that have high relevance to potential customers.

In addition, this menu can be used as a high-level customer survey to identify which issues are having the greatest impact on the customer's business environment. See Figure 8.3 for an example of a CBI Menu that might be applicable to a CRM offering. Instead of focusing on CRM product features, the menu provides a concise set of conversational entry points that can be used across marketing and sales communications. This template creates a shared point of reference for how we intend to approach customers on a problem (pain) basis. Here we also include related or similar items from the overall problem inventory, because various customers may use different terms or connect more closely with a related variation of the problem. In addition, we also include related top-of-mind trends and issues that can be helpful in creating interest.

From the example in Figure 8.3, we can see that one key component of the messaging platform should be developed around the problems and challenges that companies are facing in demand generation, versus an announcement of a new feature for campaign management software. Each item in the CBI Menu can be taken a step further into something we refer to as Solution Messaging Cards. For each of the high-level items in the CBI Menu, Solution Messaging Cards provide a "conversational template" that includes the following:

- *Customer problem.* A brief description of the problem, need, or opportunity being experienced by the customer
- *Trend relevance.* Key trends and issues in the marketplace that relate to the problem state of the customer

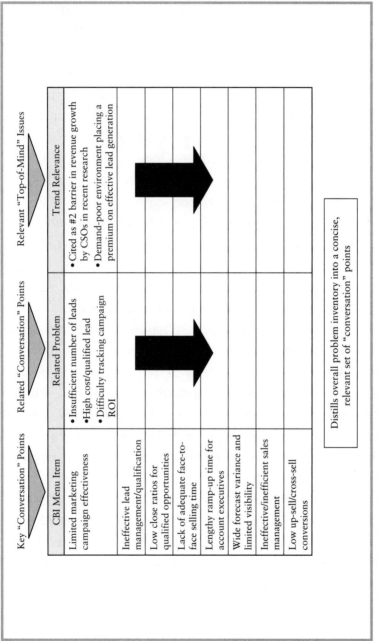

Figure 8.3   Critical Business Issue Menu Example

The figure shows a table with the following content:

CBI Menu Item	Related Problem	Trend Relevance
Limited marketing campaign effectiveness	• Insufficient number of leads • High cost/qualified lead • Difficulty tracking campaign ROI	• Cited as #2 barrier in revenue growth by CSOs in recent research • Demand-poor environment placing a premium on effective lead generation
Ineffective lead management/qualification		
Low close ratios for qualified opportunities		
Lack of adequate face-to-face selling time		
Lengthy ramp-up time for account executives		
Wide forecast variance and limited visibility		
Ineffective/inefficient sales management		
Low up-sell/cross-sell conversions		

Key "Conversation" Points

Related "Conversation" Points

Relevant "Top-of-Mind" Issues

Distills overall problem inventory into a concise, relevant set of "conversation" points

- *Cause of problem.* Specific causal factors in the customer's environment that are creating the problem situation
- *Problem impact.* Specific operational and financial impact of the problem on the customer's business
- *Required capabilities.* Capabilities required to address the specific causes of the problem
- *Metrics or proof of value.* Operational and financial metrics that can be used to determine if the problem is being successfully addressed
- *Solution linkage.* How the proposed solution fulfills the capabilities required to address the problem or need
- *Our differentiators.* Unique aspects of the solution that provide an advantage for the customer
- *Case studies.* Related case studies that demonstrate prior success in solving the problem

Figure 8.4 provides an illustration of a sample Solution Messaging Card. Each item in the CBI Menu can be expanded to create a "deck" of Solution Messaging Cards, which forms the basis for multiple downstream processes and tools.

A deck of Solution Messaging Cards for each market segment comprises a common language and frame of reference for key marketing and sales communications. Figure 8.5 illustrates how the components of the integrated value framework and messaging platform relate to one another.

Customer Problem (CBI)	Inability to determine relative effectiveness of marketing campaigns and inability to determine best use of lead generation resources
Trend Relevance	• Cited as #2 barrier in revenue growth by CSOs in recent research • Demand-poor environment placing a premium on effective lead generation
Cause of Problem	• Unable to define campaigns and track lead sources accurately • Unable to associate campaigns with costs accurately • Unable to track lead conversion to qualified opportunities • Unable to determine revenue by campaign / lead source
Problem Impact	• Difficulty setting priorities for promotional programs • High cost/qualified lead • Leads frequently discarded by sales/low conversion rates • Lower overall marketing leads/lower revenue contribution
Required Capabilities	• Ability to define multilevel campaigns/events and associated cost structures • Ability to track leads by source • Ability to track all leads by sales pipeline status and cost/revenue ratios • Ability to analyze campaign effectiveness trends
Metrics/Proof of Value	• Cost/lead • Campaign cost/lead ratios • Percent leads resulting in qualified opportunities • Realized revenue/specific campaign costs
Solution Linkage	• Campaign Builder • Lead Tracker • Campaign Pipeline Viewer • Campaign Analyzer
Our Differentiators	• Simple campaign/event linkage • All pipeline views available by campaign • Campaign analyzer provides effectiveness "index" • "What if" Scenario Modeler
Case Studies	• Software Company—increased percentage of qualified leads by 17%; improved revenue/lead by 12% • Manufacturing Firm—improved program ROI by 23%

Figure 8.4   Solution Messaging Card Example

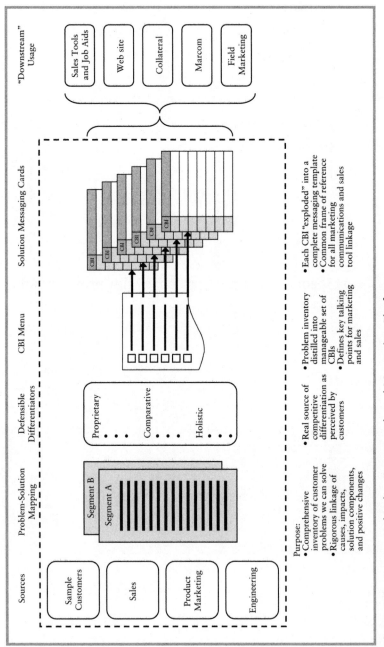

Figure 8.5 Integrated Value Framework and Messaging Platform

ASSESSMENT CRITERIA FOR THE SOLUTION MESSAGING PLATFORM

- Are key messages about problems, needs, and opportunities that customers are experiencing and relate to, versus products and services and their features?
- Do messages have "connectivity" to key trends and issues that are top-of-mind to specific buying sponsors?
- Do messages incorporate key elements of the differentiation framework?
- Do messages align closely with conversations that salespeople are striving to have with prospects and customers?
- Do messages help to create anxiety and stimulate a sense of urgency?
- Do messages allow customers to easily trace the linkage from problems they are experiencing to solutions and capabilities that you provide?
- Are messages tailored to address the critical business issues for each key market segment?
- Are messages within each market segment tailored to address the critical business issues of specific buying sponsors?

THE GO-TO-MARKET APPROACH

It is critical to carefully identify those market segments that are best served by the problems your firm actually solves.

In a demand-poor environment, it is even more critical to clearly understand the relevance and measurable impact of potential solutions to target segments.

THIS AREA OF THE HEALTH CHECK is to a large extent a validation and calibration assessment. In this stage of the diagnosis, we assess the extent to which key go-to-market assumptions are in alignment with actual problems being solved for customers.

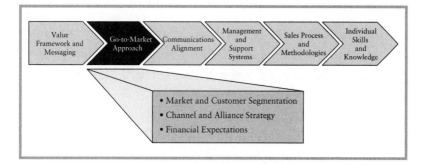

MARKET AND CUSTOMER SEGMENTATION APPROACH

It is critical to revisit the problem-solution mapping and to carefully identify those market segments that are best served by the problems we *actually* solve. In some cases, we may find that our thinking about the appropriateness of our target markets is incorrect or that alternative market segments may have significant potential. When our organization transitions from being product-centric to solution-centric, it stands to reason that some aspects of segmentation methodology might require some recalibration. The overarching purpose of segmentation is to improve the probabilities of playing where we can win. These probabilities improve significantly when the following are true:

- There is close alignment of our offerings with problems and needs of specific types of customers.
- We have the ability to communicate with high levels of relevance to potential buyers.
- We have the ability to differentiate through refined specialization or focus.

To a large extent, segmentation methodology attempts to create these advantages by applying *parameters* or variables to subdivide an overall market population. So the question is, "Based on the problems and needs we actually address, is our segmentation approach creating a unique advantage for us?" Some common segmentation parameters include the following:

- *Demographic.* Characteristics such as household composition or age. In a B2B environment, some potential parameters are number of employees, annual revenues, number of locations, and vertical industry.
- *Usage.* How offerings are applied or used in different ways by customers.
- *Benefits.* Attributes such as quality, price, service, or brand loyalty.

- *Geographic.* Buyers in certain geographic regions may share characteristics that make them receptive to certain offerings.
- *Geo-demographic.* The intersection of geography and demographics may further refine targeting capabilities.
- *Psychographics.* Mindset attributes such as attitudes, lifestyle preferences, or career orientation (in a B2B context, attributes of corporate culture or philosophy).
- *Socioeconomic.* Characteristics such as income, occupation, or education.

In many cases, segmentation decisions are based on internal or external research that indicates a high level of *product* interest for a certain demographic. While this type of research can be useful, it can also be misleading. High levels of *interest* in a certain type of product or service does not necessarily mean that customers will ultimately justify an actual purchase. Simply anticipating that your organization will win its fair share of the market can be a dangerous assumption. In a demand-poor environment, it is critical to clearly understand the relevance and measurable impact of potential solutions to target segments. That is, the segmentation "lens" should give significant consideration to how specific critical business issues relate to the segmentation variables being applied. This improves the probabilities of value "defensibility" for market segments that are identified.

In a demand-poor environment, simply assuming your organization will win its fair share of the market is dangerous.

A useful worksheet to assist with the appropriate focus on customer problems is illustrated in Figure 9.1. This CBI/Segmentation Mapping Worksheet evaluates each critical business issue across fundamental segmentation variables. The purpose of this exercise is to systematically assess the potential relevance of segmentation variables with the actual problems and needs we intend to address in target segments.

This relevancy assessment can help to refine our thinking about the appropriateness of the segmentation approach, as well as to refine specific attributes of the "ideal customer" for each segment. In addition, this approach may reveal the need to develop a more vertical

CBI Menu	Segmentation Variables				
	Benefits and Outcomes	Usage	Demographics	Psychographics	Geographics
Critical Business Issue #1	How does this CBI relate to benefits and outcome variables?	How does this CBI relate to usage variables?	How does this CBI relate to demographic variables?	How does this CBI relate to psychographic variables?	How does this CBI relate to geographic variables?
Critical Business Issue #2					
Critical Business Issue #3					
Critical Business Issue #4					
Critical Business Issue #5					

Figure 9.1 CBI/Segmentation Mapping Worksheet

orientation, because truly understanding problems and needs of customers typically requires a high degree of focus. Mohanbir Sawhney, McCormick Tribune Professor of Technology at the Kellogg School of Management, has recently written extensively on the marketing implications of a solutions focus. He notes:

> In the solutions mindset, customer offerings are integrated combinations of products and services designed to provide customized experiences for specific customer segments. Customer segments or vertical markets become the dominant axes for organization and process design.

ASSESSMENT CRITERIA FOR MARKET SEGMENTATION

- Have specific segmentation variables been defined for each target market?
- Are specific attributes defined for each segmentation variable (e.g., early adopter for psychographics)?
- Do the actual problems and needs addressed by your solutions have clear and direct relevance to the specific target market segments?
- Is the relevancy of each CBI (critical business issue) Menu item for a market segment considered and understood for each segmentation variable and its attributes?

- Is the potential value impact of each solution clearly understood and quantified on a relative scale for each target market segment?
- Are the characteristics for ideal customers formally defined, and does an ideal customer profile exist for each key solution and market segment combination (e.g., fast follower)?
- Are value framework and messaging platform and ideal customer profiles for each market segment in close alignment?
- Have all potential target market segments for solutions or solution components that you offer been identified?

CHANNEL AND ALLIANCE STRATEGY

Much like the segmentation strategy, it is critical to assess whether the channel and alliance strategy aligns with the value framework and messaging platform, as well as the market and customer segmentation approach. In the overall channel strategy, it is necessary to consider the degree to which *problem synergy* exists in various market segments and then thoughtfully assess the extent to which both direct and indirect sales channels can function in a *problem-solving* mode.

In product-centric organizations, product or capability synergies can take precedence over problem synergies in sales channel design. In other words, it can be easy to assume that products and services with similar *capabilities* can be sold to disparate types of buyers through the same sales channel. This may or may not be true depending on the situational fluency required to effectively engage with a given buying audience. We refer to this assumption as the *cross-selling misconception*. Conventional cross-selling occurs when additional or extended value can be offered to the same or similar buying constituencies. The cross-selling misconception occurs when companies attempt to sell similar offerings through the same sales channels to fundamentally *different* buying constituencies. If the fundamental problem domain and usage of the offerings are highly similar, then the channel approach can work, but if not, results can be disappointing.

Like the segmentation approach, a solutions focus tends to place emphasis on *problem* synergies as the primary lens through which other channel variables are considered. It is important to realistically consider these problem-oriented fluency requirements when formulating the direct sales channel approach. Previous approaches to channel and organizational design may not be effective as greater problem-solving literacy becomes essential. Depending on the combined segmentation/channel model, there may be significant organizational design issues in the direct sales force that we will discuss in a later section.

Indirect channels may require recalibration as well. Sales through indirect channels can be challenging as a more solutions-focused approach is pursued. The causes for this are fairly obvious; channel partners that may have been historically adept at representing product capabilities and features may struggle to function as effective problem solvers. There are two potential outcomes in this scenario: either the composition of the partner community needs to be adjusted, or solution-centric knowledge and skills transfer must be applied to the existing partner base. It is important to assess whether reseller channels have the appropriate capabilities to represent the problem-solving capabilities of your solutions. In addition, it is equally important to cull out "window dressing" alliances and focus on partners that can add value from a problem-solving perspective.

A problem-focused lens has a number of implications on overall channel design. A well-designed channel strategy can impact two key dimensions of solution-centric market success—scale and scope. Various types of "reseller" agents can significantly impact scale and cost-effective coverage into market areas that would be difficult to reach directly. Alliance partners can help to create opportunities where problem scope is broader than the solution set we provide. Figure 9.2 illustrates a template that can help to clearly identify key considerations when calibrating the channel approach for solutions.

This figure helps to guide criteria for the channel model by considering the degree to which two key factors interrelate:

- *The directness of problem-solution linkage.* This axis represents the extent to which solutions you provide directly and completely address specific problems and needs of the customer.
- *The complexity of the overall problem domain.* This axis represents the overall scope and complexity of the problems being addressed.

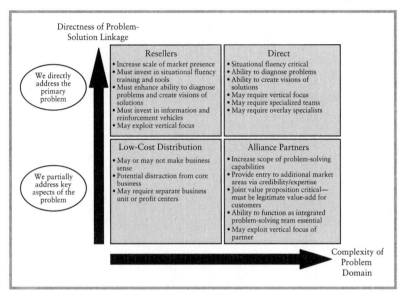

Figure 9.2   Channel Calibration Considerations

Jointly considering these two dimensions of the problem domain can provide valuable insights into the appropriate sales channel approach. It is important to continually revisit this as both market conditions change and solutions evolve.

ASSESSMENT CRITERIA FOR THE CHANNEL STRATEGY

- Does the channel strategy align with the value framework and segmentation approach (do sales channels make sense considering the types of problems being solved and the market segments being addressed)?

- Do internal sales channels have the required situational fluency skills to diagnose customer problems and needs?
- Do third-party resellers have the appropriate literacy, market focus, and reach for the targeted market segments?
- Do alliance partners legitimately add value in terms of solving customer problems—is the joint value proposition relevant and defensible at the point of sale?
- Does the overall channel model provide coverage in the appropriate segments to exploit potential demand for your solutions?
- Are channel resellers and alliance partners consistently provided with the skills and knowledge transfer required to successfully represent your offerings?
- Does the channel and alliance strategy help influence key market and customer segments by creating a pull-through effect?

FINANCIAL EXPECTATIONS

When moving to a solution-centric approach, to a large extent you are reformulating the offerings of your organization. That is, you are presenting new types of composite products and services to solve customer problems. It is important to realistically model how specific formulations of products and services that comprise solutions will make their way into the marketplace and generate revenue.

In order to accomplish this, it is essential to rationalize this new product-service mix with both the segmentation and channel model. This both serves as a sanity check and helps to define downstream accountability and performance expectations that are consistent with a solution-centric approach. In addition, it is important to resolve whether "all roads lead to quota" or whether accountability by offering a mix is necessary to either drive a solutions focus or maintain certain margin levels. Companies need to evaluate whether such a model exists, and if not, create one—how will we roll up and hold people accountable for the overall revenue forecast, considering that we're moving to solutions?

At a high level, it is important to rationalize the key dimension of the strategic revenue model, including:

- Revenue projections by segment
- Revenue projections by channel
- Revenue projections by solution mix (product and service)

Figure 9.3 provides a high-level illustration of the appropriate triangulation between these key dimensions. While the illustration is somewhat simplistic, it is important to thoughtfully rationalize how the solution-focused approach will manifest itself economically from a segmentation, channel, and offering perspective.

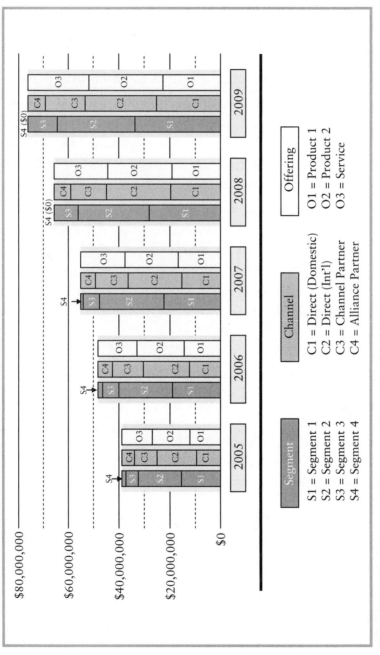

Figure 9.3 Three Revenue Views over Time—Graphical Data

ASSESSMENT CRITERIA FOR FINANCIAL EXPECTATIONS

- Are addressable market sizes and revenue targets rational and credible for specific offerings and organizational capabilities?
- Are key performance indicators defined and realistic by market segment?
- Are key performance indicators defined and realistic by sales channel?
- Are key performance indicators defined and realistic by product-service mix for solution packages?
- Are segment and channel projections rationalized with the solution product-service mix?
- Are internal and external (channel and alliance) realities factored into financial expectations for specific offerings?
- Are key performance indicators integrated into accountability and incentive planning?

COMMUNICATIONS ALIGNMENT

*All aspects of corporate communications
to the external world need to be assessed
carefully and aligned with the problems that
the organization solves—not aligned with
the products that it makes.*

Marketing departments need to seriously consider whether their campaigns launch only products or launch problem resolutions.

THIS AREA OF THE HEALTH CHECK is performed to assess the extent to which key aspects of both internal and external communications align with the problems and needs defined in the value framework and messaging platform.

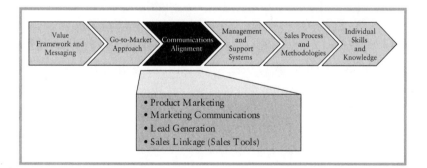

PRODUCT MARKETING ALIGNMENT

It is critical that marketing *internally* orients its communications around real problems that customers value solving and that product marketing methodologies are explicit about the links between product and service characteristics and the customer value of problems being solved. Sometimes a large addressable market may drive the erroneous assumption that certain types of products or services will capture, by default, some percentage of an overall space. In addition, many product and service priorities are often driven significantly by factors that do not necessarily relate to point-of-sales defensibility, including:

- *Engineering elegance.* Technology-related firms can become enamored with their own engineering prowess and the "cool factor." The question is, "How does this elegance explicitly relate to customer advantage?"
- *Competitive paranoia.* While it's important to be knowledgeable of the competitive environment, assuming that you must match competitive offerings feature for feature may not be a valid perspective and may not create an advantage at the point of sale.
- *Customer compelled.* Companies sometimes confuse being customer-focused with being customer-compelled. The accommodation of customer one-offs may be acceptable or necessary, but incorporating individual customer requirements into the general solution portfolio can be disruptive and unprofitable if value defensibility is not considered for the broader set of potential buyers.
- *Analyst kowtowing.* Third-party analysts may be influential in setting the requirements for offerings in specific markets. While some of their research and perspectives can be useful in determining product and service priorities, their opinions can fuel the feature/function race—both providers and buyers need to challenge the value defensibility of these perspectives.

Although developing a real understanding of potential customer value early in the solution life cycle can be a challenging process, it ensures that product and service investments can be defended successfully at the point of sale in competitive environments. The key mindset shift is to retain a problem-solving lens when formulating solutions and to continually think forward to the point-of-sales interaction in the solution definition and prioritization process.

In order to think clearly about defensible customer value, it's important to apply structure to the process and thoughtfully consider types of customer outcomes. For more on this subject, Mohanbir Sawhney has written extensively about the need to think in outcome-based terms when defining solutions. Some typical customer value drivers include the following:

- *Cost reduction.* How does the solution contribute to specific forms of reduced cost?
- *Revenue expansion.* How does the solution improve abilities to grow revenues?
- *Capital utilization.* How does the solution improve the ability to utilize capital or other assets?
- *Improved knowledge, comprehension, and insight.* How does the solution improve the ability to more effectively manage the business?
- *Risk avoidance.* How does the solution decrease the probabilities of risks that could have a negative impact on the customer's business?

- *Total cost of ownership (TCO).* How does the solution's overall characteristics result in a lower cost of ownership while solving the customer's problem?
- *Enhanced competitiveness.* How does the solution enable the customer to compete more effectively?

Creating criteria around customer value drivers can be challenging, but with some effort and collaboration, it is possible to do so for general and specific forms of customer value. Again, like other solution-centric disciplines, establishing some level of rigor is the key. Figure 10.1 illustrates an approach to objectively quantify a set of customer value drivers (the numbers are purely examples of possible quantitative measures). While not exhaustive, this example can be extended or adapted to meet the needs of specific market segments. In other words, the problem-solution mapping may reveal a number of market-specific value drivers that can significantly add to value defensibility during the sales process.

When customer value drivers have been defined and assessed for a given solution component or package, these values can be incorporated into an overall prioritization model. Figure 10.2 illustrates the integration of customer value drivers into a comparative model, where one or more solution concepts may be competing for finite capital and development resources. This model provides a comparative rating for both the market attractiveness and the cost and risk characteristics for each solution idea. In addition, the model then computes an attractiveness/investment index. The absolute value of this index pro-

Value Impact			
Cost reduction impact	☐ > $50K/year potential ☐ $5K–$20K/year potential	☐ $20K–$50K/year potential ☐ No impact	
HOW?:			
Revenue expansion impact	☐ > $500K/year potential ☐ $50K–$100K/year potential	☐ $200K–$500K/year potential ☐ No impact	
HOW?:			
Capital utilization impact	☐ > $500K/year potential ☐ $50K–$100K/year potential	☐ $200K–$500K/year potential ☐ No impact	
HOW?:			
Risk avoidance	☐ 3+ examples	☐ 1–2 examples	☐ No examples
HOW?:			
Total cost of ownership impact	☐ > 5% impact to implementation/maintenance goals	☐ > 1%–4% impact to implementation/maintenance goals	☐ No impact
HOW?:			
Enhanced competitiveness	☐ 3+ specific examples	☐ 1–2 specific examples	☐ No examples
HOW?:			

Figure 10.1 Customer Value Driver Worksheet

vides clues as to which solution ideas have the best pay-back probabilities. Note that customer value driver variables in this example comprise 25 percent of the overall score for the solution ideas that are under consideration. While there is no perfect weighting scheme for each of the comparison categories, giving a relatively high weight to customer value drivers can help illuminate which solution ideas may have the greatest customer impact.

By comparing the market opportunity to the overall investment and risk characteristics of each solution concept shown in Figure 10.2, we can also readily construct a

	Weight	Idea 1 Score	Value	Idea 2 Score	Value
Customer Value Drivers					
Cost reduction	5	High	25	Medium	15
Revenue expansion	5	Medium	15	Medium	15
Capital utilization	5	High	50	Medium	30
TCO impact	3	Low	3	Low	3
Enhanced competitiveness	5	High	50	Medium	30
OVERALL VALUE DRIVER IMPACT	25%		35.75		23.25
Customer Dynamics					
Perception of value	5	Medium	15	Medium	15
Buying sponsor relevance (related to pain)	4	High	20	High	20
Educational complexity	2	High	–10	Low	–2
OVERALL CUSTOMER DYNAMICS IMPACT	5%		1.25		1.65
Market Dynamics					
Scope of addressable market (how many potential customers)	4	High	20	High	20
					(continues)

Figure 10.2 Solution Investment Comparative Model

	Weight	Idea 1 Score	Value	Idea 2 Score	Value
Market growth rate	3	Low	3	Low	3
Market maturity (less mature is positive)	4	High	20	High	20
Barriers to entry	4	Low	4	Low	4
Ability to create awareness	3	Medium	9	Medium	9
Relevance to key market trends	2	High	10	Medium	6
OVERALL MARKET DYNAMICS IMPACT	15%		9.9		9.3
Revenue Characteristics					
Existing customers/ time-to-revenue	5	High	25	Low	5
Revenue growth rate	4	High	20	High	20
Margin characteristics	4	High	20	Low	4
Revenue stream longevity/ recurrence	10	High	50	Medium	30
OVERALL REVENUE IMPACT	10%		11.5		5.9
Competitive Landscape					
Existence of established competition	4	Low	−4	Medium	−12
Market penetration by competitors	5	Low	−5	Low	−5
Differentiation of solution	4	Medium	12	Medium	12
OVERALL COMPETITIVE IMPACT	20%		0.6		−1
Feasibility					
Technical feasibility	5	High	25	High	25
Predictability of outcomes	4	Medium	12	High	20
Organizational feasibility	4	High	20	Medium	12
Strategic fit	5	High	25	High	25
OVERALL FEASIBILITY IMPACT	10%		8.2		8.2
Investment/Infrastructure Requirements					
Capital requirements	10	Low	−10	High	−50
Marketing resources	3	Medium	−9	Medium	−9
Engineering resources	4	Medium	−12	Low	−4
					(continues)

Figure 10.2 *Continued*

■ **183** ■

	Weight	Idea 1 Score	Value	Idea 2 Score	Value
Sales resources	3	Low	–3	High	–15
Educational/training investment	3	Medium	–9	Medium	–9
Intellectual capital/expertise (resident in-house knowledge)	4	Low	–4	Low	–4
Overall risk	10	Low	10	High	–50
OVERALL INVESTMENT/ INFRASTRUCTURE IMPACT	15%		–4.622		–11.43
TOTAL SCORE	100%		62.578		35.868
Attractiveness Total			67.2		47.3
Investment Index			–4.62		–11.43
ATTRACTIVENESS/ INVESTMENT INDEX			–14.5		–4.1

Figure 10.2 *Continued*

portfolio view of potential opportunities. Figure 10.3 provides a comparative view of five solution ideas that are "competing" for internal resources. This view allows us to visualize the market attractiveness of the idea versus the overall cost/risk characteristics. A positioning in the upper-right quadrant would indicate a high market attractiveness with relatively low investment risk characteristics. In addition, the bubble size allows us to see a relative ratio of market attractiveness to cost/risk.

From a solution-centric perspective, if we apply a high weighting to the customer value driver criteria in Figure 10.2, the portfolio view can illustrate which solution ideas will most likely connect the best with customer needs and problems during the marketing and sales process.

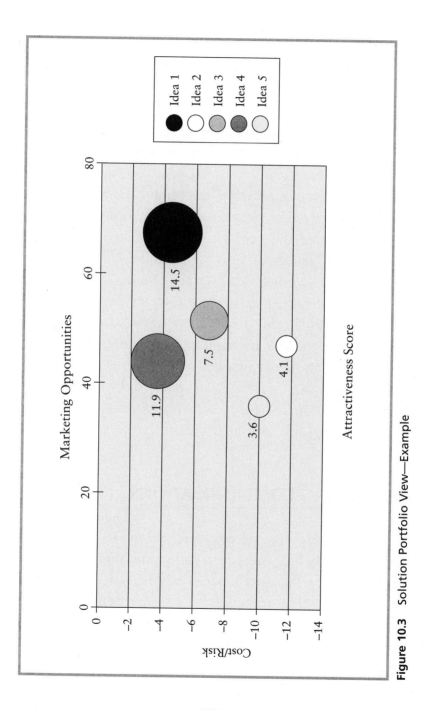

Figure 10.3 Solution Portfolio View—Example

ASSESSMENT CRITERIA FOR PRODUCT MARKETING ALIGNMENT

- Do overall product marketing methods begin with a well-defined problem-solution mapping as a foundation?
- Do internal marketing communications vehicles, such as market requirements definitions (MRDs), incorporate the problem-solution mapping extensively to define solution opportunities?
- Are rigorous methods in place to assess and define customer value potential for each solution concept?
- Is defensible value a significant variable in the overall prioritization methodology for solution offerings and their enhancements?
- Are solution packages as defined by marketing explicitly linked to customer problems and needs and to specific customer outcomes?

MARKETING COMMUNICATIONS

All aspects of corporate communications to the external world need to be assessed carefully and aligned with the problems that the organization solves, not aligned with the products that it makes. Customer perceptions are formed by the multiple forms of communications from your organization, all of which need to be consistent and in parallel (Figure 10.4).

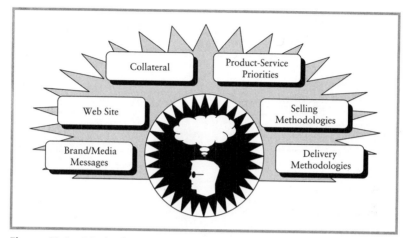

Figure 10.4   Marketing Communications—Customer Perception

Web sites, Marcom collateral, white papers, analyst presentations, and other media relations activities, advertising agency campaigns, and all messaging projects—in fact, any decision on how and what will be communicated to the external world in any medium or channel—ought to be consistent with real customer problems that are solved and actual needs that are addressed. In other words, we need to make it as easy as possible for customers to know if we identify with them and the problems they are experiencing.

As mentioned earlier, the Solution Messaging Cards for each market segment provide the overall frame of reference for consistent communications through all channels, as illustrated by Figure 10.5.

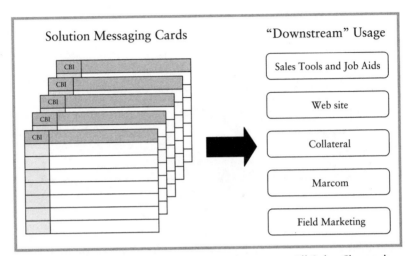

Figure 10.5 Consistent Solution Messaging across All Sales Channels

ASSESSMENT CRITERIA FOR MARKETING COMMUNICATIONS

The corporate Web site, collateral, and all forms of external communications should be reviewed with respect to the following criteria:

- Do communications focus initially on the problem state facing the customer—the specific problems, needs, and challenges the customer is often experiencing?
- Are the causal factors or drivers for these problems identified clearly (the internal and external forces that are actually creating the existing problem state for the customer)?

- Is the business impact of problems, from both an operational and financial perspective, clearly linked to the causes of problems?
- Are the consequences of not addressing the problem or need identified (or the consequences of delay)?
- Are the specific capabilities required to address the actual *causes* of the problem state clearly articulated?
- Is it easy for the customer to understand how the solution provides the needed capabilities to address *causes* of the problem state?
- Do advertising and media communications focus extensively on compelling customer problems and critical business issues?
- Do white papers, articles, and thought leadership vehicles apply a problem-focused lens?
- Are each of the preceding items tailored for specific market segments and associated buying sponsors?

LEAD GENERATION

In many cases, marketing campaigns and lead generation efforts are based on the release of a product or service, as opposed to the new abilities to solve customer problems. In order to generate qualified opportunities on a consistent basis, lead generation vehicles should focus on the problems that salespeople should be exploring with customers as they attempt to uncover areas of real customer need. In other words, are lead generation initiatives launching problems or launching products?

ASSESSMENT CRITERIA
FOR LEAD GENERATION

- Do lead generation vehicles consistently align with the value framework and messaging platform?
- Do campaigns focus on customer problems and themes from the CBI Menu (versus product releases and updates)?
- Do lead generation activities align with market segments and critical business issues specific to each segment?
- Do lead generation activities incorporate specific top-of-mind issues at the buying sponsor level?
- Are lead generation roles and responsibilities clearly defined and integrated between marketing and sales?
- Are there clear qualification criteria for lead filtering and turnover to salespeople?
- Do salespeople have the requisite levels of situational fluency to effectively follow up on qualified leads generated by marketing?
- Have salespeople been trained in specific techniques for effective prospecting?
- Are leads tracked by problem type?

SALES LINKAGE AND SALES TOOLS

It is critical that essential elements of the solution messaging platform make their way into practical sales tools that the field sales organization and channel organizations can use. If making this translation is not taken seriously, all the hard work upstream of the sales process goes to waste. Salespeople will be less capable of creating interest and communicating the differentiated value of your company's solutions. It is important to review sales tools and ensure that key aspects of the solution messaging platform are consistently being applied in the field.

As with marketing communications, the Solution Messaging Cards for each segment provide a common frame of reference for input into essential sales tools as depicted in Figure 10.6.

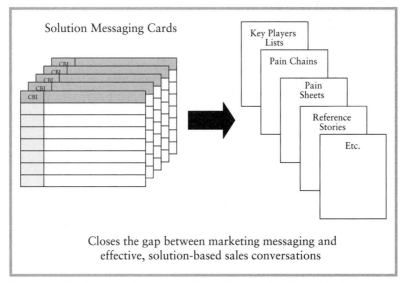

Figure 10.6 Solution Messaging Cards Supporting Sales Tools

ASSESSMENT CRITERIA FOR
SALES LINKAGE AND SALES TOOLS

- Have Key Player Lists, Pain Chains, and Differentiation templates been created that reflect critical business issues and key aspects of the solution messaging platform?
- Are relevant Value Propositions and Reference Stories available for key problems and needs that we address?
- Are Situational Fluency Prompters created for each market segment and buying sponsors that we are targeting?
- Are value justification tools in place for each distinct solution offering?

MANAGEMENT AND SUPPORT SYSTEMS

When selling solutions, the ability to coach and mentor is highly dependent on the presence of a common and well-defined sales process.

Sales management is the first line of support in reinforcing desired sales force behaviors.

THIS AREA OF THE HEALTH CHECK provides an assessment of how well sales management and support systems effectively reinforce solution-centric practices and principles. In this context, the term *system* refers to the broad spectrum of policies, procedures, and technologies that reinforce operational goals.

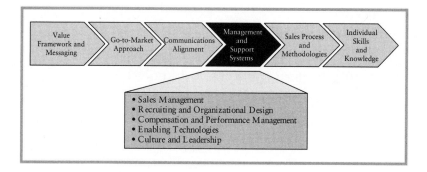

SALES MANAGEMENT

Sales management should be highly capable of leading, motivating, and coaching salespeople to continuously improve sales performance and achieve other strategic goals. When selling solutions, the ability to coach and mentor is highly dependent on the presence of a common and well-defined sales process.

ASSESSMENT CRITERIA
FOR SALES MANAGEMENT

- Do sales managers have the requisite knowledge and skills to be effective coaches and mentors for the sales force (i.e., situational knowledge, business acumen, solution-centric messaging, and consultative selling skills)?
- Do sales managers have and use a defined sales management process?
- Is the sales management process integrated with the organization's common sales process?
- Does the sales management process provide the ability to perform a detailed analysis of sales pipelines?
- Does the sales management process provide the ability to perform a detailed analysis of individual sales opportunities?
- Does the sales management process provide the ability to help salespeople close immediate "must win" sales opportunities?
- Can sales managers use the analysis of pipelines and opportunities to identify sales skill deficiencies and improve them over the long term?
- Does the sales management process provide accurate and timely reporting of sales results, including forecast accuracy?
- Does the sales management system support effective execution of territory, account, and opportunity man-

agement methodologies, such that resources are consistently deployed to the highest-value opportunities?

- Does the sales management system facilitate a team selling environment?
- Does the sales management system clearly articulate and measure sales performance standards?
- Do sales managers use hiring profiles and consistently hire and retain high-performing salespeople?
- Does the sales management system measure the activities that produce results, and not just end results alone?
- Does the management system help to focus attention and activity on maximizing client results and not exclusively on internal financial gain?

Sales management is the first line of support in reinforcing desired sales force behaviors. To provide effective coaching and mentoring, sales management needs to be highly educated and literate in all Solution Selling disciplines, including territory management, account planning, strategic opportunity management, and sales execution. Figure 11.1 provides a sample of a sales management flowchart that encompasses the requisite management skills.

RECRUITING AND ORGANIZATIONAL DESIGN

In many cases, the hiring profiles and aptitudes of the existing sales organization need to be recalibrated to ensure that salespeople can diagnose business problems

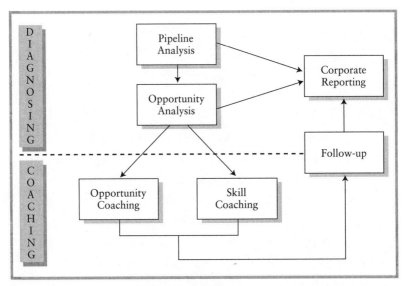

Figure 11.1 Sales Management Flowchart

and sell solutions effectively. As McKinsey has suggested, "Typically, less than a third of a product-oriented sales force can make the necessary transition [to a solution-centric one]. Successful solutions organizations often replace more than 50 percent of their existing product sales force in the first 12 months." While we may not agree with this level of replacement, some level of transformation will be necessary to transition to a solution-centric organization.

> Less than a third of a product-oriented sales force can make the transition to a solution-centric one.

In addition, you may have to change your organizational structure in order to support solution-centric operations. For example, your organizational design may need to be adjusted to provide the necessary level of problem-solving specialists to support your sales team. You may need to implement a matrix approach or other means of coordinating specialist resources often demanded for solution-centric sales.

ASSESSMENT CRITERIA FOR RECRUITING AND ORGANIZATIONAL DESIGN

- Do your recruiting criteria include situational knowledge, business acumen, solution-centric messaging, and consultative selling skills—all required to support solution-centric sales?
- Do your recruiting criteria include the sales candidate's ability to gain access to executives and have executive-level dialogues?
- Do you evaluate salespeople's ability and track record to stimulate and create interest?
- Do your recruiting criteria include the sales candidate's ability to use enabling technology effectively?
- Is there a structured hiring process that involves interviewers from sales and other departments (e.g., marketing or service delivery)?
- Is there a structured training process for new hires that optimizes training time-to-productivity and time-to-proficiency—including a formal mentoring process?

- Do job descriptions exist that include criteria for solution-centric skills, knowledge, and behavior for all positions being recruited?
- Does the organizational design include specialists to assist the sales team in the diagnosis of customer problems?
- Does your organizational structure allow the sales team to assemble and apply virtual resources commensurate to the size of each opportunity or account, as required?
- Are rules of engagement, including roles, accountabilities, and decision rights clearly articulated and understood?
- Is each manager's span of control narrow enough to provide for coaching and development of his or her direct reports?
- Are specific liaisons or points of integration identified between marketing, sales, and customer service?
- Does the organizational structure enhance interdepartmental and intradepartmental communications and sharing of best practices?
- Does the reporting structure of the organization enhance interdepartmental alignment and accountability (i.e., is there a single executive responsible for marketing and sales integration)?

COMPENSATION AND PERFORMANCE MANAGEMENT

Compensation and measurement are the keys to behavioral change and performance for any sales force—what gets measured gets done. Compensation and incentives should reinforce the execution of solution-centric activities and reward the attainment of goals that align with selling solutions.

ASSESSMENT CRITERIA FOR COMPENSATION AND PERFORMANCE MANAGEMENT

- Do sales incentives encourage desired activities that support solution-centric behavior (e.g., adhering to the sales process and proficiency in required skills and knowledge)?
- Do you reward people based on *customer* outcomes and value attainment versus solely internal metrics?
- Do you measure and reward salespeople's ability to define customer business problems, assess the impact of customer business problems, and define the value of problem resolution in an opportunity?
- Do salespeople participate in the development of quotas or sales goals?
- Does territory potential factor into the setting of sales quotas?

- Do 70 percent or more of your sales team members reach or exceed their sales goals?
- Do your compensation and incentive plans include profitability or margin goals?
- Are your sales goals aligned with corporate objectives for the product and services mix that comprise your solutions?
- Are market factors such as average total direct compensation considered in the development of your compensation plans?
- Are performance standards documented, communicated, and measured?
- Are performance plans developed at least annually with every employee?
- Are poor performers removed?

ENABLING TECHNOLOGIES

Technology can be a substantial barrier or a powerful enabler to transform your organization into a solution-centric team. The key is to recognize that technologies should *enable* people and processes to function more effectively and efficiently as a problem-solving organization. The key dimensions for enabling technology are process support, knowledge management, collaboration, and performance measurement.

ASSESSMENT CRITERIA FOR ENABLING TECHNOLOGIES

- Is your sales process supported by the enabling technology used by your sales team?
- Does your enabling technology help you to execute the right activities to move opportunities through the sales process?
- For each sales opportunity, does your enabling technology track the completion of verifiable outcomes for each step in the sales process?
- Does the completion of sales process steps determine sales forecast probabilities?
- Does your technology support the efficient creation, distribution, and sharing of Solution Selling job aids (e.g., Solution Messaging Cards, Pain Sheets, Pain Chains, Key Player Lists, Reference Stories, and Success Criteria)?
- Does your technology enable your sales team to find the business problems that you have previously helped to solve?
- Does your technology enable your sales team to articulate the value that specific customers received from your solutions?
- Does technology support the sharing and consistent use of value messages for your solutions?
- Do technologies reduce administrative burdens that keep salespeople from selling?

- Do enabling technologies facilitate alignment and collaboration between marketing, sales, fulfillment, and service processes?
- Does technology enable virtual teams to collaborate in real time on active opportunities and accounts?
- Does your technology help salespeople to configure a potential solution to customers' business problems?

CULTURE AND LEADERSHIP

Organizational culture and leadership are the ingredients that hold the organization together and give it life. Uninspired leadership at the corporate, regional, and local levels will weaken sales force morale and significantly lower the probability of sustaining behavioral change. When undertaking a significant organizational transformation, the executive team and managers all need to be evangelists and enforcers of the new direction. If the leadership team fails to display genuine commitment to the stated direction, it is quickly written off as just the latest management "flavor of the month."

Becoming solution-centric requires
the commitment and inspiration
of the senior management team.

ASSESSMENT CRITERIA FOR CULTURE AND LEADERSHIP

- Is your organization's culture dynamic (i.e., open to change, resilient, and willing to take risks)?
- Does the culture and behavior of the management team reflect genuine commitment to the transformation to a solution-centric organization?
- Does the leadership team understand the six distinct approaches to leadership and skillfully switch between the styles based on the situation?
- Are individual contributors who are promoted to management positions given management training and mentoring?

SALES PROCESS AND METHODOLOGIES

When asked, most executives will claim that their organization has a defined sales process. However, we find that organizations often confuse sales process *with the nomenclature in their sales funnel or with the steps provided by the CRM or sales automation systems they are using.*

*Management disciplines that support
sales processes include opportunity, account,
and territory management.*

THIS AREA OF THE HEALTH CHECK provides an assessment of sales process and methodologies that are critical to ensure consistent sales performance and the transformation to a solution-centric organization. A company's sales process and enabling methodologies should be aligned with the customer buying process.

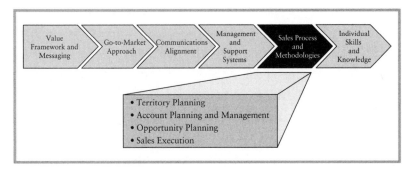

SALES PROCESS

We are often asked, "Why have a sales process?" The simple answer is that it provides everyone involved in the sales effort a roadmap of what to do next, which leads to a higher probability of success. After all, few sales campaigns today are orchestrated by a single individual. And it doesn't matter if your sales cycles are single-event transactions or a series of events over a long period of time.

Knowing what to do and when to do it is critically important to success.

By definition, a *process* is a systematic series of actions, or a series of defined, repeatable steps to achieve a result. When followed, these steps can consistently lead to expected, verifiable outcomes. A sales process defines and documents those end-to-end steps that lead to increased sales performance. Many people think of sales processes only in the context of sales execution, but this is too limited a view. An effective sales process should encompass planning on the front end and implementation on the back end as well.

When asked, most executives will claim that their organization has a defined sales process. However, we find that organizations often confuse *sales process* with the nomenclature in their sales funnel or with the steps provided by the CRM or sales automation systems they are using. Not only do these so-called sales processes fail to include the critical functions of planning or implementation, they almost never include the enabling sales methodologies. In situations like this, sales process is actually a myth.

Management disciplines that support sales processes include opportunity, account, and territory management. Figure 12.1 depicts the alignment of major elements of sales planning, execution, and implementation in the context of these management disciplines.

The sales process must align with the customer's buying process. An example of this is illustrated in Figure 12.2. Because so many other aspects of the sales process (i.e.,

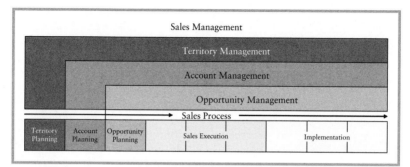

Figure 12.1 Sales Process and Methodologies with Management Disciplines

activities, outcomes, roles, job aids, and probability of winning) are a function of the customer's buying process, misalignment between these dimensions will impede sales performance.

In order to operate successfully, the sales process must also be aligned with a supporting management system. This system should provide sales managers with a structured approach toward their activities in support of the sales process. For example, in the area of strategic business planning, the sales management system should guide managers in goal setting, establishing quotas, assigning accounts, and defining territories. Further, the sales management system should also provide managers with a clear, structured approach for diagnosing their business pipelines, coaching sales opportunities, and developing salespeople. The frequency of these activities will vary depending upon the rhythm and cadence of the business as defined by the kinds of customers served and the solutions provided.

| Develop business strategy & define/execute initiatives | Determine needs/ requirements | Evaluate alternatives | Select solutions & evaluate risk | Resolve issues & finalize contracts | Implement & evaluate success |

Sales Process Steps

Plan			Execute						Implement
					Sales Execution				
Territory Planning	Account Planning	Opportunity Planning	Create	Qualify	Develop	Prove	Negotiate	Close	Implement
Annually	Quarterly	As required			Weekly				Ongoing

Sales Process Activities

- **Territory Planning:** • Determine prospect requirements • Identify qualification criteria • Grade, rank and segment accounts
- **Account Planning:** • Assess account • Define current business • Identify new opportunities • Prioritize opportunities • Select initial accounts
- **Opportunity Planning:** • Assess opportunity • Analyze organizational support, role coverage, role and influence • Select initial competitive strategy
- **Create:** • Identify potential sponsor • Stimulate interest • Reassess opportunity and competitive strategy
- **Qualify:** • Define sponsor's pain • Create or reengineer vision for sponsor • Gain agreement to explore • Negotiate access to power • Confirm on next steps
- **Develop:** • Define power sponsor's pain • Create or reengineer vision for power • Gain agreement to explore • Determine evaluation criteria • Suggest next steps • Confirm dialogue/agree upon next steps
- **Prove:** • Execute next steps • Present preliminary solution • Conduct review of proposal • Ask for the business • Issue proposal • Receive verbal approval
- **Negotiate:** • Prepare for final negotiations • Reach final agreement
- **Close:** • Get necessary documents signed
- **Implement:** • Implement solution • Measure success criteria • Identify potential new opportunities

Verifiable Outcomes

- Territory Planning: • Territory Plan
- Account Planning: • Account Plan
- Opportunity Planning: • Opportunity Plan
- Create: • Interest stimulated
- Qualify: • Sponsor Letter
- Develop: • Evaluation Plan
- Prove: • Verbal approval
- Negotiate: • Ts & Cs agreed upon
- Close: • Signed documents
- Implement: • Implementation Plan

Roles (examples)

- Territory: • Sales • Sales mgt. • Sales support
- Account: • Sales • Sales mgt. • Sales support
- Opportunity: • Sales • Sales mgt. • Sales support
- Create: • Sales • Marketing
- Qualify: • Sales • Sales mgt.
- Develop: • Sales • Sales mgt.
- Prove: • Sales support
- Negotiate: • Sales • Sales mgt.
- Close: • Sales • Sales mgt.
- Implement: • Sales support • Sales

Job Aids

- Territory: • Territory Plan
- Account: • Account Plan
- Opportunity: • Opportunity Plan • Opportunity Assessment • Competitive Strategy Selector
- Create: • Value Proposition • Reference Story • Bus. Dev. Letter • Bus. Dev. Prompter
- Qualify: • 9 Block Model™ • Plan Sheet™ • S. A. Prompter • Sponsor Letter
- Develop: • 9 Block Model™ • Plan Sheet™ • S. A. Prompter • Sponsor Letter
- Prove: • Evaluation Plan • Transition Letter • Implement. Plan • Value Analysis • Success Criteria
- Negotiate: • Negotiating Worksheet • Give-Get List
- Implement: • Implementation Plan • Success Criteria • Reference Story

Sales Management System

Territory	Qualified Suspect	Qualified Sponsor	Qualified Power	Decision Due	Pending Sale	Win
0%	10%	25%	50%	75%	90%	100%

Business and Strategic Planning
- Goal and quota setting
- Account assignment
- Resource planning

Team Development:
- Performance
- Recruiting
- Training

Figure 12.2   Sales Process Map with Management Considerations

ASSESSMENT CRITERIA FOR THE SALES PROCESS

- Have you defined your customers' buying process for each type of solution you provide?
- Have you defined and documented the selling steps for your solutions?
- Are the steps in your selling processes aligned with how your customers buy?
- Does your sales process include steps for both planning as well as sales execution?
- Are the sales activities defined for each step in the sales process?
- Does the sales process clearly delineate roles, responsibilities, and accountabilities?
- Is your sales process supported by job aids that accelerate opportunities through the sales funnel?
- Are verifiable outcomes linked to customer behaviors defined for each step in the sales process?
- Do you determine the probabilities of winning business based upon the attainment of verifiable outcomes within your sales process?
- Is your sales forecast aligned with completion of sales activities within the sales process?
- Does the management system support the consistent use of the defined sales process?
- Are selling processes relevant to the various sales situations (e.g., complex or transactional) that salespeople find themselves in on a routine basis?

- Are the points of integration (inputs and outputs) between your sales process and other organizational departments or functions defined (e.g., marketing to sales or sales to customer service)?
- Do your enabling technologies, such as CRM, support the execution of your sales process?

SUPPORTING METHODOLOGIES

A sales process requires enabling methodologies at each step. Just as an automobile assembly line represents the steps of a process, how the car is assembled at each step represents the use of methodologies. Process steps determine *what* needs to happen—methodologies define *how* each step will be accomplished. Essential methodologies for supporting sales process include:

- Territory planning
- Account planning
- Opportunity planning
- Sales execution

Territory Planning Methodology

Effective territory planning is an extension of the overall segmentation strategy. In most cases, there are more potential suspects in a territory than salespeople can engage with in a given time period. Therefore, it is critical to apply a structured process to ensure that the highest-potential targets in territories are being targeted by the sales organization. Effective use of selling resources requires application of the following territory planning disciplines:

- Accurately determining the number of prospecting contacts needed to make the quota
- Prioritizing the accounts in the territory according to specific qualification criteria
- Segmenting the prioritized list to identify the most promising prospects
- Developing a territory coverage strategy for all accounts in the territory
- Effectively using information resources to gather essential intelligence about the accounts in the territory
- Developing an approach to initiate sell cycles in the high-priority accounts

Execution of these disciplines is possible only when salespeople have a firm understanding of the markets they serve and a solid appreciation for which potential customers are most receptive to their company's value messages.

A useful tool to apply in territory planning is the Account Prioritization Matrix, which evaluates territory prospects against a set of defined attractiveness criteria. This tool, an example of which is illustrated in Figure 12.3, helps salespeople to prioritize their assigned accounts by relevant criteria. Salespeople should spend the most time in opportunity development with those accounts that score highest in the heaviest-weighted criteria.

Account Name	Our revenue from this account last year		Strategic value to us	Our solution fit to their needs	Growth in revenues	Customer satisfaction level	Urgency of pains	sort
	Normal	High	High	Normal	High	Normal	High	Ranked index
CaughmanBakers	8		4	8	20	7	18	65
M$A Payroll Services	7		18	6	14	10	8	63
Kwik Transport	9		16	9	10	10	8	62
Matchmakers, Inc.	10		18	9	2	8	12	59
TJM Charities	0		18	8	12		20	58
Kelley-Alan Travel	8		12	6	4	9	14	53
Blalock Consulting Group	8		14	6	0	6	12	46
Lifestyle Leasing	0		16	10	14		4	44
4Square Entertainment	0		16	4	6		18	44
City Government	4		10	6	0	6	8	34
								0

Figure 12.3   Territory Planning: Account Prioritization Matrix

ASSESSMENT CRITERIA
FOR TERRITORY PLANNING

- Do salespeople know which accounts are their responsibility to cover?
- Do salespeople know which accounts are customers?
- Do salespeople know the amount of business from current customers in their assigned accounts?
- Are the highest-potential prospects identified and prioritized?
- Are prioritization criteria standardized and consistently applied?
- Does each member of your sales team know how many prospecting contacts are required to achieve his or her sales quota?
- Do members of your sales team have access to high-quality information about accounts assigned to them, which they can use to evaluate prioritization criteria?
- Are your budgets and quotas established or defined in whole or in part by your territory planning methodology?
- Are territory plans updated on a regular basis?

Account Planning and Management Methodology

The costs and complexities of selling to and managing large accounts are rapidly increasing. The transition to solution selling can provide a broader customer "footprint" potential, but in order to achieve this, the need for effective account planning takes on much greater significance. "Harvesting" additional revenues requires investment in higher levels of account knowledge and continual understanding of key customer business initiatives. Support of the customer's strategy is crucial to its success and to the success of the sales team. In addition, managers should be able to prioritize opportunities and properly allocate resources.

An effective account planning methodology addresses these issues through a systematic application of analysis and collaboration. Account planning requires application of the following disciplines:

- Identifying the business issues confronting an account and the associated value for addressing those issues
- Aligning the critical business issues with the appropriate key players in the account
- Identifying the specific solutions that your organization can bring to help the account solve its business problems
- Understanding where and how decisions are made in the account
- Aligning your sales resources with the key players in the account to ensure optimum coverage
- Developing a competitive strategy for penetrating and developing business in the account
- Dynamically managing account information in order to better adapt sales actions to changing customer requirements

Effective account planning and management requires a deep understanding of a customer's internal decision-making processes. This knowledge is only possible when a salesperson has established productive relationships up and down the customer's formal and informal organizational hierarchy. A useful tool for effective planning involving account relationships is the Account Planning Coverage Summary, as illustrated by Figure 12.4.

ASSESSMENT CRITERIA FOR ACCOUNT PLANNING AND MANAGEMENT

- Does your sales team regularly research the critical business issues in accounts?
- Does your sales team understand the current business initiatives of accounts?
- Can your organization share important account information in a structured, orderly fashion?
- Is the information known about accounts a driving factor in setting your company's goals, quotas, and budgets?
- Is there a structured approach to identify and act on potential opportunities within established accounts?
- Does your sales team employ a structured method for prioritizing potential opportunities in accounts and for allocating sales resources to those opportunities?
- Do we understand the lines of influence between key individuals in an account?

COVERAGE SUMMARY

Name	[x] = Sr. Exec	Title [x] = Senior Executive	Business unit division	Level of: C	Level of: S	Role F	Role I	Influence By:	Influence Over:	Team member assigned	Potential pain	Competitor present Y	Competitor present N
Smith, Jim	x	CFO	Operations	1	?	FI		Watts	Smith	Gomez	Poor cash flow		N
Jones, Steve	x	VP Sales	S&M	3	3	UA	PS	Smith	Ricks	Hart	Declining sales revenue		
Moore, Donna	x	COO	Operations	2	2	OP		?	?	Hart	Increasing operational costs		
Watts, John		CIO	Operations	0	?	TK		?	Smith	Zizzi	Difficulty supporting LOB	Y	
Ricks, Jane		VP Marketing	S&M	3	2	OP	S	Jones	?	Hart	Poor return on campaigns		
Brown, Chris		VP HR	Operations	0	?	AP		Smith	?	TBD	Difficulty hiring desired talent		

(C) Contact
(S) Support:
(F) Formal role:
(I) Informal role:

0 = none, 1 = low, 2 = medium, 3 = high;
0 = none, 1 = low, 2 = medium, 3 = high; ? = unsure, X = adversary
UA = ultimate authority, FI = financial, LE = legal, OP = operational,
AP = admin./purchasing, TK = technical, ? = unsure
[S] = sponsor, [PS] = power sponsor

Figure 12.4 Account Planning Coverage Summary Example

- Is there a standard way in which an account team constructs and delivers a value "report card" to senior management within an account?
- Is there an effective mechanism for measuring customer satisfaction in accounts and responding to any satisfaction shortcomings?
- Does the sales team develop and execute effective competitive strategies to win business in accounts and protect account relationships?
- Is the account team providing thought leadership (strategic value) to the customer?

Opportunity Planning Methodology

In every organization's sales pipeline, there are some opportunities that are larger and more critical to achieving sales goals. These must-win opportunities typically require more resources to win, and they require repeated contacts with multiple people in the customer account over a longer period of time. Since these kinds of opportunities entail a higher degree of complexity, planning the most effective allocation of direct and virtual sales resources is essential to winning. Winning in these situations is a team sport and requires effective coordination of many moving parts—internally and externally.

In this regard, opportunity planning takes on similar aspects as account planning. Both account planning and opportunity planning develop actions for the sales team to engage with individuals in accounts to win business. Both opportunity planning and account planning help develop an understanding of the external factors that will impact the decision that a customer will ultimately make—such as business drivers, competitive alternatives, and political influences in the customer's decision-making process.

Opportunity planning straddles both account planning and sales execution methodologies. A key aspect of opportunity planning is the definition of *what* actions and tactics need to be done to win the opportunity. *How* those actions are performed falls within the domain of sales execution methodology. No matter how good a plan to win an opportunity may be, it is of no value unless you can execute the actions in your plan to produce results. Therefore, an effective opportunity planning methodology must link to and align with your sales execution methodology—the *what* of your plan is realized in the *how* of your sales team's actions.

Like account planning, an effective opportunity planning methodology addresses these issues through a systematic application of analysis and collaboration. Opportunity planning requires application of the following disciplines:

- *Assessment.* Can we realistically compete and win?
- *Competitive strategy.* Which competitive approach has the best chance for success?
- *Organizational alignment.* Do we fully understand how influence, power, and politics will affect the customer's decision?
- *Proof of value.* Can we rigorously define and defend measurable value for our solution?

- *Resource planning.* Are we applying our resources in the right places, at the right time, and with the right people?

Opportunity planning is enhanced through the use of enabling tools, such as the Opportunity Assessment Worksheet shown in Figure 12.5. This tool enables members of the sales team to determine if they should compete in an opportunity and to reassess their competitive position as they progress through a campaign.

ASSESSMENT CRITERIA FOR OPPORTUNITY PLANNING

- Are win rates acceptable on large or high-value opportunities?
- Are opportunity qualification standards defined, understood, and followed?
- Is it okay in your organization to qualify out of an opportunity?
- Are competitive strategies for winning opportunities defined, communicated, and tactically executed?
- Are the customer's organizational influence, power, and politics identified within large or high-value opportunities?
- Is the sales team effective in navigating the political landscape of the buying organization?

Opportunity Assessment Worksheet

Answer key: Yes, No, or Unsure
★ = "Quick 5" assessment questions

Assessment date: ____

		Us	Competition
★	**PAIN—"Is the customer likely to act?"**		
1	Has high priority pain or potential pain been identified?		
2	Have we validated the pain with the owner(s)?		
3	Do we understand how others are impacted by the pain?		
4	Is there a budget in place?		
5	Is there a timeframe to address the pain?		
★	**POWER—"Are we aligned with the right people to win?"**		
6	Do we understand the roles of the key players for this opportunity?		
7	Do we understand who will influence the decision and how?		
8	Are we connected to the people in power?		
9	Do we have the support of the key players?		
10	Are we connected to the people with access to funds?		
★	**VISION—"Does the customer prefer our offering?"**		
11	Did we help establish the initial requirements?		
12	Does our offering fit their needs/requirements?		
13	Have we created or reengineered a differentiated vision for the key players?		
14	Do the key players support our solution approach?		
★	**VALUE—"Does our offering provide mutual value?"**		
15	Do we understand the benefit to each key player/corporate?		
16	Have the key players quantified and articulated the benefits of our offering to us?		
17	Has a (corporate) value analysis been agreed upon?		
18	Does the value analysis warrant access to funds?		
19	Is there sufficient value to us? Profitable? Strategic?		
★	**CONTROL—"Can we exert control over the buying process?"**		
20	Do we understand the decision-making process and criteria for the key players?		
21	Do we understand the proof and satisfaction requirements for the key players?		
22	Do we understand the customer's buying practices, policies, and procedures?		
23	Has the customer agreed to an evaluation process with us?		
24	Can we control the evaluation process?		
25	Can we successfully manage our risk?		

Figure 12.5 Opportunity Assessment Worksheet

224

- Do you have a method for assigning company executives to buying companies' executives within large and high-value opportunities?
- Can the sales team differentiate its solutions from competitive and other alternatives?
- Is your cost of sales in line with company expectations?
- Are sales team resources utilized optimally in pursuing opportunities?
- Do sales team members (especially virtual team members) collaborate effectively?
- Does the sales team know consistently whether it is winning or losing a sales opportunity?

Sales Execution Methodology

While territory, account, and opportunity planning can help to determine what a sales team must do in order to attain its goals, ultimately the team must also know how to perform those actions. However, there are many ways in which a sales team can execute tactically, and not all of them are effective. A sales execution methodology provides sales teams with a pattern of behavior that is based on the best practices of top performers.

The components of an effective sales execution methodology include:

- Stimulating the interest of potential buyers
- Defining and diagnosing business problems

- Creating visions of solutions in the minds of buyers
- Getting access to influential and powerful people
- Determining the value of a solution to a buyer
- Managing proof of value of solutions
- Negotiating and closing sales
- Measuring the customer's success

A sales execution methodology enables your sales team to facilitate each step within the sales process. This includes defining both the specific activities in each step and how they will be accomplished, as illustrated in Figure 12.6. As a result, sales managers can use the sales execution methodology as a standard for coaching. Further, they can accurately determine the potential for winning business in their sales funnel.

ASSESSMENT CRITERIA FOR SALES EXECUTION

- Do your salespeople consistently execute all the required steps to close business?
- Does your sales team stimulate or create buyer interest in your offerings and capabilities?
- Does your sales team have job aids and tools to enable it to create new opportunities?
- Do your salespeople identify and diagnose business problems of potential customers?

Milestone	Yield	Milestone description	Activities
T	0%	TERRITORY	☐ Opportunity identified in territory
S	10%	QUALIFIED SUSPECT	☐ Meets marketing criteria ☐ Potential Sponsor identified ☐ Initial contact established (verifiable)
D	25%	QUALIFIED SPONSOR	☐ Pain admitted by Sponsor ☐ Sponsor has a valued buying vision ☐ Sponsor agreed to explore ☐ Sponsor granted access to power ☐ Agreed to above in Sponsor Letter
C	50%	QUALIFIED POWER SPONSOR	☐ Access to Power Sponsor ☐ Pain admitted by Power Sponsor ☐ Power Sponsor has a valued buying vision ☐ Power Sponsor agreed to explore ☐ Evaluation Plan proposed ☐ Evaluation Plan agreed upon
B	75%	DECISION DUE	☐ Evaluation Plan under way ☐ Preproposal review conducted ☐ Asked for the business ☐ Proposal issued, decision due* ☐ Verbal approval received
A	90%	PENDING SALE	☐ Contract negotiation in progress
W	100%	WIN	☐ Signed documents
			☐ Update prospect database

* Premature delivery of a proposal is NOT a sign of progress.

Figure 12.6 Pipeline Milestones

227

- Does your sales team attempt to sell solutions, not just product features and functionality?
- Does your sales team get access to the appropriate levels of customer organizations, where buying decisions are made?
- Does your sales team have the situational knowledge and business acumen to diagnose the critical issues of customers?
- Do your salespeople routinely get something in return for their actions (e.g., they don't discount, provide demos, or make concessions unnecessarily)?
- Do your salespeople sell value at every stage of the sales process (i.e., they lead, qualify, and close based on the value of solutions)?
- Does your average sales cycle close in the amount of time that your organization expects?

INDIVIDUAL SKILLS AND KNOWLEDGE

Buyers want a consultant who is going to add value to their situation. Otherwise, buyers could just go to a Web site for product information and price quotes. Today, salespeople must possess the relevant skills and knowledge to add value in every sales situation—otherwise, they won't survive.

Top-performing salespeople integrate situational knowledge, capability knowledge, people skills, and selling skills to develop situational fluency— the ability to interact consultatively with buyers and add value in every sales situation.

THIS AREA OF THE HEALTH CHECK is conducted to ensure that sales professionals have the appropriate skills and knowledge to sell solutions effectively. A skill is the individual's ability to perform activities at a proficiency level sufficient to successfully complete the required steps in the sales process. Mastery of skills alone is insufficient for sales success, however. Just as a highly skilled surgeon with little understanding of anatomy is a prescription for disaster, salespeople must also possess the right knowledge so they can apply their skills at the right time, with the right people, and in the right ways.

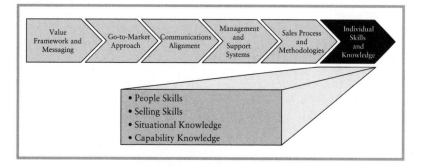

Unfortunately, some stereotypes continue to influence many people's perception of the sales profession, such as the tragic figure of Willy Loman in Arthur Miller's play *Death of a Salesman*: "He's a man way out there in the blue, riding on a smile and a shoeshine." The erroneous belief that many salespeople can succeed solely through superficial—even disingenuous—interpersonal skills is certainly not true today, if it ever really was.

Good interpersonal skills are certainly important to sales success, but they are no longer sufficient by themselves. Several recent studies of executive-level buyers' opinions show that they want to do business with salespeople who really understand them. They want to talk with salespeople who have a complete understanding of their situation as well as a good working knowledge of the capabilities necessary to help them solve their problems.

If you ask sales managers what they look for in their salespeople, they'll often reply that they seek proven selling skills; they want "great closers." They look for people with successful selling track records. However, in order to sell solutions to customer problems, not just products, salespeople need much more than the ability to close business.

Good closers may not make the best salespeople in the solution-centric organization.

What buyers clearly don't want are pushy salespeople interested only in selling their products and services. Buyers want a consultant who is going to add value to their situation. Otherwise, buyers could just go to a Web site for product information and price quotes. Today, salespeople must possess the relevant skills and knowledge so they can add value in every sales situation—otherwise, they can't survive.

Figure 13.1 illustrates how top-performing salespeople integrate situational knowledge, capability knowledge, people skills, and selling skills to develop situational fluency—the ability to interact consultatively with buyers and add value in every sales situation. Effective salespeople know how to integrate their people and selling skills with capabilities knowledge and with broader knowledge of the customer's marketplace and environment in order to conduct credible sales conversations. They are able to relate to specific problems and needs in the customer's world and to discuss critical business issues and challenges fluently with buyers.

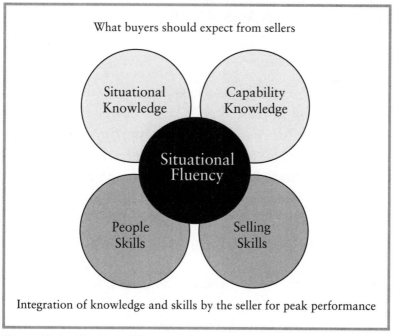

Figure 13.1   The Four Elements of Situational Fluency

SITUATIONAL KNOWLEDGE

Effective salespeople seek first to understand their customers' problems before expecting the customers to understand their company's offerings. In order to do this well, salespeople need to know about their customers' business—both the internal operations of the business and the external factors that affect the business. This is similar to a doctor understanding how a particular patient's body functions and the environmental factors that may be affecting that patient.

ASSESSMENT CRITERIA
FOR SITUATIONAL KNOWLEDGE

- Do salespeople have access to information sources to remain abreast of the latest customer business trends, industry factors, and competitive threats?
- Do salespeople have adequate understanding of customer marketplace issues and trends to converse credibly with buyers, especially high-ranking ones?
- Do salespeople have the ability to converse confidently with executive buyers about specific issues in their businesses?
- Do salespeople consistently demonstrate knowledge of the business issues that exist within buyers' industries, companies, and positions?

- Do salespeople recognize symptoms of common business issues for their customers and know how to diagnose and verify the causes of these symptoms?

CAPABILITY KNOWLEDGE

To be effective, salespeople need to be sufficiently familiar with the capabilities of their offerings—as well as any other relevant capabilities available in the market—to the extent that they can identify which solution components are most important in a specific customer's situation.

The ability to create the logical linkages from problems to solution capabilities is the essence of *vision creation* or *vision reengineering*. These key skills enable salespeople to help other people see how they can solve their problems. In order to win business, salespeople must have the ability to help customers create their vision of a solution or reengineer their existing visions to ones that favor the capabilities provided by the salesperson.

ASSESSMENT CRITERIA
FOR CAPABILITY KNOWLEDGE

- Are salespeople able to consistently link customer needs with specific capabilities?
- Do salespeople communicate defensible differentiators effectively when discussing their capabilities?

- Are salespeople able to clearly articulate how a potential buyer can attain a goal through the use of their capabilities?
- Can salespeople consistently enable customers to envision themselves using your company's unique capabilities to solve their problems?
- Are salespeople capable of delivering a concise "elevator pitch" about the value of your organization's capabilities?
- Are salespeople capable of delivering "proof" messages that validate the value of your company's capabilities?
- Do salespeople understand other relevant capabilities (beyond your own) that also help solve your customers' business problems?

While capabilities knowledge is definitely a requirement for developing situational fluency, there is a danger in overinvesting in this kind of training. By focusing too much on product training—to the detriment of the development of situational knowledge, people skills, or selling skills—some organizations will reinforce product-focused selling behavior. The ability to recite every feature and function of a given product or service can be useful, but not if customers can't see how these capabilities help them to solve their problems.

Therefore, capabilities knowledge alone is not sufficient to ensure good sales performance—salespeople must be able to integrate this knowledge with other elements of situational fluency in order to position and sell solutions to customer business problems. Effective salespeople are capable of coherently mapping their company's solutions to a customer's problems. They are capable of positioning the tangible value of their solutions as more than the simple bundling of multiple product offerings.

PEOPLE SKILLS

The ability to successfully develop and maintain interpersonal interactions and relationships is a vital skill for sales success. In general, people buy from people they like. To this end, a salesperson's ability to develop rapport with buyers, and to develop empathy for customers' situations, can be a great help in winning business.

However, research on buyer behavior shows that this is less true today. In fact, buyers often won't buy from salespeople they like if the salespeople can't provide the best solutions to their problems. Today, people skills alone are insufficient to sustained success in sales. The best-performing salespeople not only have good people skills but have also integrated these with other aspects of situational fluency.

ASSESSMENT CRITERIA FOR PEOPLE SKILLS

- Do your salespeople build genuine rapport with customers?

- Do your salespeople understand how to adapt their behavior and selling style to a variety of buyer personality types?
- Do salespeople exhibit empathy for customers' problems and demonstrate an innate desire to solve them?
- Do your salespeople understand the psychological aspects of how buyers buy?
- Do salespeople understand how to negotiate and close business without jeopardizing the business relationship?

SELLING SKILLS

One of the by-products of defining a sales process is that the skills required to successfully execute each step of the process can be clearly identified and prioritized. A complete sales process requires mastery of a wide variety of selling skills, including:

Sales planning and management skills
- *Sales management skills.* For managers, the ability to plan, analyze, and coach effective sales behavior and to develop salespeople's skills and abilities over time
- *Territory analysis and planning skills.* The ability to correctly determine which accounts should be prioritized for sales activity and for ensuring sufficient coverage of assigned accounts
- *Account analysis and planning skills.* The ability to penetrate targeted accounts, develop a higher level

of relationship, and protect against competitive encroachment

- *Opportunity analysis and planning skills.* The ability to coordinate and apply virtual sales resources to win competitive sales campaigns

Sales process execution skills

- *Prospecting skills.* The ability to identify likely customers and stimulate their interest and curiosity
- *Alignment skills.* The ability to demonstrate situational fluency with buyers and add value in every customer interaction
- *Value selling skills.* The ability to position the value of solutions with customers, in every step of the sales process
- *Vision creation skills.* The ability to help customers envision themselves using your capabilities to solve their problems or to reengineer their previous visions to one that favors your solutions
- *Qualifying skills.* The ability to determine whether to engage in or disengage from a sales opportunity
- *Executive access skills.* The ability to access and develop credibility with high-ranking buyers
- *Proof management skills.* The ability to demonstrate the viability and value of your solutions' capabilities
- *Sales control skills.* The ability to facilitate and influence the buyers' evaluation and selection process
- *Negotiation skills.* The ability to come to an equitable agreement with buyers
- *Closing skills.* The ability to successfully secure a buyer decision in your favor

Implementation skills

- *Customer satisfaction skills.* The ability to set realistic customer expectations and to meet them consistently
- *Success leverage skills.* The ability to communicate and get credit for the value you deliver to customers, and to develop a higher level of relationship as a result

The number of selling skills, and their relative importance, will vary according to the sales process established, the role of the salesperson, and the kinds of solutions provided. A transactional inside salesperson, for example, will have different sales skill requirements than a field sales representative selling strategic goods and services because their sales processes, while similar in many respects, will have different degrees of emphasis and timing. The best-performing salespeople are those who understand the requirements of their individual sales process and who focus on those skills required to execute every aspect of that process.

ASSESSMENT CRITERIA FOR SELLING SKILLS

- Can salespeople execute all aspects of their sales process consistently?
- Can salespeople develop effective plans for managing their territory, accounts, and/or opportunities?

- Can sales managers accurately assess their salespeople's pipelines, opportunities, and skill gaps?
- Do salespeople conduct effective precall planning and research prior to engaging in opportunities?
- Can salespeople diagnose customer problems?
- Can salespeople effectively navigate a customer organization and engage with people with sufficient influence and authority to buy?
- Can salespeople position the value of their solutions effectively?
- Can salespeople stimulate the interest and curiosity of prospective buyers?
- Can salespeople demonstrate situational fluency with buyers and add value in every customer interaction?
- Can salespeople help customers envision themselves using your capabilities to solve their problems or to reengineer their previous visions to one that favors your solutions?
- Can salespeople quickly and accurately determine whether to engage in or disengage from a sales opportunity?
- Can salespeople access and develop credibility with high-ranking buyers?
- Can salespeople demonstrate the viability and value of your solutions' capabilities?
- Do salespeople consistently facilitate and influence their buyers' evaluation and selection process?
- Do salespeople close business in the time frames they expect?

- Do salespeople negotiate equitable agreements with customers, without excessive concessions, discounts, or special terms and conditions?
- Do salespeople leverage past successes to initiate new opportunities?
- Do salespeople use internal company resources effectively?
- Are customers satisfied that the expectations set by your salespeople are being met or exceeded consistently?

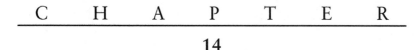

ORGANIZATIONAL IMPLICATIONS

*The health check provides a comprehensive
view of the systemic barriers to becoming
a solution-centric organization.*

A key element in transforming to a solution-centric organization is understanding the implications on certain roles.

In Chapters Eight through Thirteen, we provided you with a health checklist for each element of the Sales Performance Improvement Framework. The health check covers virtually every facet of sales performance in your entire organization, and it provides a comprehensive view of the systemic barriers to becoming a solution-centric organization.

This review of the elements of sales performance represents one dimension of solution-centric transformation. An additional dimension that should be considered is the organizational implications of transforming, including the roles and activities of different functional areas in your organization and how they support the solution-centric model.

In Chapter Seven, we presented a map of organizational involvement in the six key performance drivers of the Sales Performance Improvement Framework (shown again in Figure 14.1).

In the following tables, we review each of the six systemic drivers and the roles and accountabilities of each functional area. These tables can provide a starting point for reviewing and defining specific organizational accountabilities as your organization makes the transformation from being product-centric to solution-centric. The specific definitions of roles and responsibilities in your organization

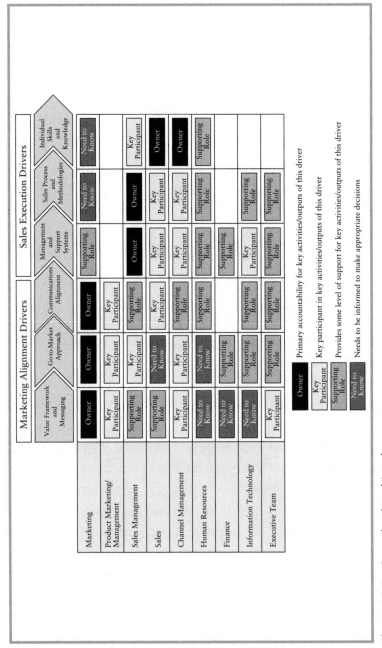

	Marketing Alignment Drivers			Sales Execution Drivers		
	Value Framework and Messaging	Go-to-Market Approach	Communications Alignment	Management and Support Systems	Sales Process and Methodologies	Individual Skills and Knowledge
Marketing	Owner	Owner	Owner	Supporting Role	Need to Know	Need to Know
Product Marketing/Management	Key Participant	Key Participant	Key Participant			
Sales Management	Supporting Role	Key Participant	Supporting Role	Owner	Owner	Key Participant
Sales	Supporting Role	Need to Know	Key Participant	Key Participant	Key Participant	Owner
Channel Management	Key Participant	Key Participant	Supporting Role	Key Participant	Key Participant	Owner
Human Resources	Need to Know	Need to Know	Supporting Role	Supporting Role	Supporting Role	Supporting Role
Finance	Need to Know	Supporting Role		Supporting Role		
Information Technology	Need to Know	Supporting Role	Supporting Role	Key Participant	Supporting Role	
Executive Team	Key Participant	Supporting Role	Supporting Role	Supporting Role	Supporting Role	

Owner — Primary accountability for key activities/outputs of this driver

Key Participant — Key participant in key activities/outputs of this driver

Supporting Role — Provides some level of support for key activities/outputs of this driver

Need to Know — Needs to be informed to make appropriate decisions

Figure 14.1 Organizational Involvement

may vary from these recommendations depending on your company size, your industry, how you are organized, and how you define your functional areas.

Value Framework and Messaging

Functional Area	Organizational Involvement and Accountabilities
Marketing	*Owner.* Plays the dominant role in defining the overall value framework and messaging platform for the company. Accountabilities include: • Defining the problem-solution mapping • Defining the Differentiation Framework • Defining the Critical Business Issue Menu • Defining Solution Messaging Cards
Product marketing/ management	*Key participant.* Plays the key role in the development of the value framework and messaging platform; works closely with strategic marketing and messaging teams to ensure that solution formulation is aligned with customer needs and problems.
Sales management	*Supporting role.* Needs to fully understand and validate the overall value proposition and messaging platform. Needs to have high literacy to effectively coach and mentor the sales team and be a successful "evangelist."

Functional Area	Organizational Involvement and Accountabilities
Sales	*Supporting role.* Key representative in the development of the value framework and messaging platform; needs to provide frontline perspectives to validate key elements of the platform; needs to illuminate new problems and needs being experienced by customers, as well as have competitive intelligence.
Channel management	*Key participant.* Needs representation in the value framework and messaging definition; needs to provide input specific to channel requirements and fully understand fluency and skills requirements in specific channels.
Human resources (HR)	*Need to know.* Needs to fully understand the core value proposition and ensure that HR practices create an appropriate environment.
Finance	*Need to know.* Needs to fully understand the core value proposition and positioning of the company in the marketplace.
Information technology (IT)	*Need to know.* Needs to fully understand the core value proposition and positioning of the company in the marketplace.
Executive leadership	*Key participant.* Needs to fully understand the core value proposition and position in the marketplace and participate in the creation of the vision; must

Functional Area	Organizational Involvement and Accountabilities
	have a clear consensus on key messages, differentiators, and the purpose of the company.

Go-to-Market Approach

Functional Area	Organizational Involvement and Accountabilities
Marketing	*Owner.* Primary player in the definition of the overall segmentation and channel strategy; accountabilities include: • Ensuring that overall segmentation, sales channel, and alliance strategies are aligned with the problem-solution mapping • Defining specific market targets and segments • Identifying key segmentation variables and relevance of critical business issues to segmentation variables by market segment • Identifying key trends and issues by segment and their correlation to critical business issues • Creating ideal customer profiles within each market segment
Product marketing/ management	*Key participant.* Needs to work closely with strategic marketing to rationalize solution fit to target market segments;

Functional Area	Organizational Involvement and Accountabilities
	needs to help rationalize overall strategic revenue model.
Sales management	*Key participant.* Needs to provide input and validate market segmentation and channel strategy; needs to participate in financial expectations and associated metrics.
Sales	*Need to know.* Needs to clearly understand market targets and implications on territory planning and management at the individual level; needs to understand where key partners and alliances can be leveraged as "opportunity multipliers."
Channel management	*Key participant.* Works closely with strategic marketing in the definition of overall segmentation and channel strategy.
Human resources	*Need to know.* Needs to understand HR implications of the overall go-to-market strategy.
Finance	*Supporting role.* Needs to provide input and feedback on strategic revenue model, metrics, and assumptions; needs to support appropriate reporting and informational needs to monitor key performance indicators (KPIs) and revenue forecasts; needs to support development and validation of pricing models for solutions.

Functional Area	Organizational Involvement and Accountabilities
Information technology	*Supporting role.* Needs to understand and support overall technology requirements for target marketing and sales channel resources (direct and indirect).
Executive leadership	*Supporting role.* Needs to provide oversight, validation, and support of the overall go-to-market strategy.

Communications Alignment

Functional Area	Organizational Involvement and Accountabilities
Marketing	*Owner.* Primary player in the propagation of solution-centric communications, both internally and externally; accountabilities include:

- Clearly communicating problem-solution mapping and differentiation information to product marketing/management

- Ensuring that solution-centric messaging is being applied consistently across all external communications channels, including Web site, collateral, media and advertising, and white papers

- Ensuring that all marketing communications consistently inform and parallel actual sales conversations

- Ensuring that effective sales linkage occurs by creating Solution Selling

Functional Area	Organizational Involvement and Accountabilities
	tools and templates that are driven from Solution Messaging Cards
	• Ensuring that lead generation campaigns focus on customer problems and needs, versus products and services
Product marketing/ management	*Key participant.* Applies problem-solution mapping extensively in the formulation of solutions; factors value defensibility heavily into prioritization models for solutions; works closely with strategic marketing to understand customer value factors versus investment costs and feasibility.
Sales management	*Supporting role.* Validates overall messaging relevance; ensures that effective sales tool linkage and marketing handoffs are taking place; ensures that the messaging platform is being translated into specific sales messages and conversation templates.
Sales	*Key participant.* Provides input to problem understanding and messaging relevance at the point of sale; provides competitive intelligence; participates extensively in sales tool linkage and job aid development.
Channel management	*Supporting role.* Provides business problem and messaging validation for

Functional Area	Organizational Involvement and Accountabilities
	channel market areas; ensures that appropriate marketing programs are in place to support solutions; ensures that appropriate solutions knowledge transfer is taking place for channel resources.
Human resources	*Supporting role.* Needs to understand internal communications requirements and ensure that appropriate vehicles are in place to build high levels of corporate literacy and consensus.
Finance	*Limited involvement.*
Information technology	*Supporting role.* Needs to understand and support technology requirements for both internal and external communications; needs to understand key knowledge management requirements for effective problem solving across sales, marketing, and engineering/solution development; needs to support outbound communications capabilities (Web site, marketing campaigns, lead management).
Executive leadership	*Supporting role.* Needs to function as a key internal and external evangelist of overall value proposition and the corporate "story."

Sales Management and Support Systems

Functional Area	Organizational Involvement and Accountabilities
Marketing	*Supporting role.* Marketing management needs to ensure that formal collaboration and handoffs are occurring between marketing and sales.
Product marketing/ management	*Limited involvement.*
Sales management	*Owner.* Primary player to ensure that appropriate management and reinforcement systems are in place to support Solution Selling effectiveness; key accountabilities include:

- Providing effective mentoring to the sales force and implementing formal reinforcement vehicles and practices to maintain the knowledge and skills abilities of the salespeople

- Applying sales recruiting practices that are designed to attract and hire problem-solving skill sets

- Developing sales compensation and reward structures that reinforce desired solution-centric behaviors and customer value attainment

- Ensuring that technology is used to enhance the ability of salespeople and teams to diagnose customer problems and create a coherent vision of the solution

Functional Area	Organizational Involvement and Accountabilities
	• Establishing metrics and KPIs to inspect and reinforce processes, behaviors, and skills • Instilling cultural and leadership practices that reinforce the desired behaviors and outcomes
Sales	*Key participant.* Needs to participate extensively in definition and requirements understanding for support and reinforcement vehicles; needs to apply and leverage all aspects of the overall support and reinforcement environment and provide ongoing feedback.
Channel management	*Key participant.* Needs to ensure that appropriate vehicles are in place to support and reinforce channel requirements, including knowledge and skills education, technology integration, and collaboration capabilities.
Human resources	*Supporting role.* Needs to help in the development and refinement of hiring practices to recruit and develop a cadre of effective solution salespeople; needs to participate in development of performance evaluations and competency models aligned with Solution Selling; needs to ensure that ongoing training and development programs are in place for knowledge and skills retention and growth; must provide input into compensation and reward practices

Functional Area	Organizational Involvement and Accountabilities
	designed to reward desired solution-centric behaviors by sales and marketing; must participate in organizational design and structure changes to enable solution-centric behavior.
Finance	*Supporting role.* Needs to approve modification of pricing and legal processes and procedures to enable solutions; needs to understand and participate in development of compensation and rewards practices.
Information technology	*Key participant.* Participates in defining the information architecture and resources required for the business to support solutions-centric business practices; works closely with marketing and sales to ensure that technology supports problem-solving capabilities of the organization; works to create improved continuity and collaboration between marketing and sales; stays current on promising enabling technology applications that can support problem-solving capabilities and solutions-centric business processes.
Executive leadership	*Supporting role.* Ensures that the corporate culture reflects the desired market positioning and genuine solution-centric approach; ensures that the overall leadership team is educated and qualified to lead the transition to solutions.

Sales Process and Methodologies

Functional Area	Organizational Involvement and Accountabilities
Marketing	*Need to know.* Needs to understand Solution Selling methods and how to effectively support the sales process and methodology.
Product marketing/ management	*Limited involvement.*
Sales management	*Owner.* Primary owner of overall sales process and methodology; key accountabilities include:

- Ensuring that the sales process is formally defined, understood, and followed and that selling processes are aligned with customer buying processes

- Enforcing structured methods for territory planning that extend from the segmentation model and that focus sales time on high-probability targets

- Implementing formal account planning and management methods that maximize strategic account yields

- Implementing effective opportunity management methods that allow teams to successfully navigate complex sales situations

- Defining clearly defined roles, responsibilities, and rules of engagement to implement the sales process and support effective team collaboration

Functional Area	Organizational Involvement and Accountabilities
Sales	*Key participant.* Needs to clearly understand and execute the sales process in alignment with customer buying processes; needs to understand and apply territory, account, and opportunity management methodologies; needs to understand roles and rules of engagement and to effectively leverage resources.
Channel management	*Key participant.* Needs to participate in the sales process definition and develop applications of the sales process to channel partners; needs to provide education and tools to channels to help in the process and methodology implementation.
Human resources	*Supporting role.* Works closely with sales to implement job designs that align with the deployed process and methodology.
Finance	*Limited involvement.*
Information technology	*Supporting role.* Needs to work with sales management, sales, and channel management to ensure that enabling technologies support the sales process and methodology.
Executive leadership	*Supporting role.* Needs to exhibit management commitment to process and methodology adoption.

Individual Skills and Knowledge

Functional Area	Organizational Involvement and Accountabilities
Marketing	*Need to know.* Needs to understand specific skills and knowledge capabilities required at the point of sale.
Product marketing/ management	*Limited involvement.*
Sales management	*Key participant.* Must ensure investment in educational and reinforcement vehicles to develop and maintain high skill and knowledge levels; needs to ensure that appropriate reinforcement vehicles are in place and utilized to sustain performance improvements.
Sales	*Owner.* Primary player in development of skills and knowledge required to effectively position and sell solutions; key accountabilities include: • Development of fundamental skills and capabilities required to diagnose customer problems and navigate the sales process • Development of exceptional situational fluency in target markets • Development of capabilities knowledge that allows for mapping of solutions to specific customer problems • Development of fundamental personal skills to build rapport with customers

Functional Area	Organizational Involvement and Accountabilities
	• Development of knowledge of the customer's marketplace and challenges to converse credibly with buying sponsors
Channel management	*Owner.* Primary player to ensure that channel partners can effectively represent solution offerings in target markets; accountabilities include:
	• Ensuring that channel managers and partner sales representatives are equipped with the fundamental skills and capabilities required to diagnose customer problems and navigate the sales process
	• Ensuring that partner selection criteria are compatible with problem-solving skills required for market success
Human resources	*Supporting role.* Ensures that learning strategy and supporting curriculum are based on job designs; ensures that appropriate skills profiles are used in the recruiting process.
Finance	*Limited involvement.*
Information technology	*Limited involvement.*
Executive leadership	*Limited involvement.*

In Part Four, we provided a detailed set of assessment criteria and tools that can be used by your organization to evaluate where potential sales performance gaps may exist. Through this analysis, you will be better able to determine how to transform your organization from being product-centric to solution-centric.

Afterword

LAST YEAR, ONE OF US, ROBERT KEAR, was having lunch with Rob Slee, who was in the final stages of writing the book *Private Capital Markets*—the most comprehensive book of its type ever compiled. Rob is clearly one of the preeminent experts in the world today with respect to global capital markets. Our discussion turned to the topic of globalization and its potential impact on corporations and their future performance and value.

After I related the difficulties that product-centric companies are experiencing in the post-2000 economic environment to Rob, we jointly concluded that many, if not most, of the corporations in today's marketplace underestimate the pace and impact that globalization will play over the next 5 to 10 years. This observation was underscored, rather emphatically, by the State of the World Forum, a nonprofit organization working for sustainable globalization, when it commented, "Globalization will change the world as radically in the 21st Century as democratization changed it in the 20th Century."

Like other major shifts throughout history, globalization will create new opportunities, markets, and wealth, but it will also create new forms of disruption and disorder in the marketplace. In essence, what we are beginning to witness is democratization of opportunity that extends to every corner of the world—one that will produce new winners and new losers. The near-instantaneous movement of information and fluidity of capital removes many traditional barriers to entry into a wide array of market opportunities that can harness enormous workforce capacities.

These factors, in conjunction with the "commoditization of knowledge" (mentioned in Chapter Two) have many companies on edge—and rightfully so. Not only are they struggling to get back to pre-2000 levels of revenue and sales performance, they are increasingly fearful of becoming commoditized and marginalized in their markets. In fact, being perceived as a commodity is one of the most frequently encountered issues in our work with large companies—which leads us to the topic of solutions.

The post-2000 world has ushered in a new marketing and sales environment. The unsettling reality of this world is this: As daunting as the challenge of sustained, profitable growth has been historically, the future offers an even more brutally competitive landscape. Companies that have marketed and sold commodity products successfully for decades will likely come under increasing pressure to provide new forms of customer value—in the form of meaningful solutions that squarely address customer problems, needs, and opportunities in innovative ways. In essence, becoming a problem-solving organization will be an integral aspect of survival for a much broader range of industries. Commodities will be recognized rapidly as such, and pseudo-solutions will be quickly exposed for the marketing jargon that they really are.

The question to honestly ask in your company today is, "Are we truly a problem-solving organization?" The depth of this question extends to the core of your identity as a company—confronting the brutal and honest truth about how your existence as a business is transformational to your customers. In Part Two of this book, we have strived to provide criteria and principles that can help your organization to objectively answer this question. A second, but equally important question to pose is this: "Is your organization *systemically* aligned to connect with real customer problems and needs on a consistent, repeatable basis?" This systemic capability is what we view as *solution-centric*, and it is our genuine belief that companies that can holistically develop this problem-solving acumen will be the winners in their markets. In Parts Three and Four of this book, we have outlined a framework and introduced concepts and methods that we hope will provide a significant jump start in your efforts to transition to being solution-centric.

Finally, it is important to recognize that at this point in time, the overall transition from products to real solutions is in its infancy for the large majority of companies. No framework is perfect, and no concepts apply universally to all situations. In this book, we have tried to find a starting point for companies to begin a meaningful transition from being product-centric to solution-centric. Over the next several years, as we work with more companies who are genuinely pursuing this transformation in various industries, there will certainly be much greater evolution and refinement of thought in this area. What is important is that companies transform the notion that "everyone is a salesperson" from being a cliché into something that is consciously woven into the accountabilities of each area of the organization.

While we certainly wish you luck in your endeavors, more importantly, we wish you well in rationally managing the probabilities of success—and we hope that this book is a material contributor to that end.

Index

About the Authors

In a career spanning more than thirty years, Keith M. Eades has provided an innovative framework and enhanced marketing and sales productivity for top performing, global organizations including IBM, Microsoft, and Manpower. He is the founder, chairman, and senior managing partner of Sales Performance International (SPI), a leading authority on marketing and sales performance improvement. Currently doing business in over fifty-four countries, SPI has grown into one of the largest sales improvement companies in the world under Eades' leadership and was recognized by the *Charlotte Business Journal* Fast 50 in 2002 for exceptional growth.

Eades is the best-selling author of *The New Solution Selling* (McGraw–Hill, 2004) and coauthor of *The Solution Selling Fieldbook* (McGraw–Hill, 2005) and *The Solution-Centric Organization* (McGraw-Hill, 2006).

A graduate of Clemson University, Eades received Clemson's Alumni Fellow Award in 2001 for his outstanding career accomplishments. He is an adjunct professor at Clemson and an inaugural member of the Shapiro Center Entrepreneurial Round Table.

Eades currently serves on the board of directors at Connexus, a corporate performance improvement and innovation firm, and on the executive advisory board at Clemson University College of Business.

Robert E. Kear has over twenty-five years of extensive, hands-on experience in all facets of technology industry management, including marketing, sales methodology, software engineering, professional services delivery, and P&L accountability. His last corporate position was vice president of marketing strategy and CRM strategy for JD Edwards & Company, where his role was the development of CRM strategy and deployment of methodologies to drive value-based marketing disciplines.

From 1994–2001, Kear was the cofounder and chief strategy officer of YOUcentric, an enterprise customer relationship management (CRM) software company, where he was responsible for all aspects of corporate strategy, market planning and execution, and product direction. In 2001, Kear was awarded Carolinas' Ernst & Young eBusiness Entrepreneur of the Year. From 1987–1994, Kear served as manager of client/server business systems for Cedalion Systems, where his responsibilities included all aspects of general management and P&L responsibility, with a focus on strategic planning, business development, and sales automation implementation. Kear's formative experience includes technology and management positions at Broadway & Seymour, ITT Telecom, and Wrangler. Kear holds advanced and undergraduate degrees in mathematics from East Carolina University.